HOW TREAT
A WOMAN

The Professional Man's
Guide to Achieving
Meaningful Relationships
with Women of the Modern Era

Gary Knight

Knight International

How to Treat a Woman
The Professional Man's Guide to Achieving Meaningful Relationships with Women of the Modern Era
All Rights Reserved.
Copyright © 2008 Gary Knight
V6.0

ISBN: 978-0-615-15319-3

Dedicated to my darling Brenda
Whose reaction when she read this book was:
"I shouldn't have married you so fast!"

Foreword

This is not a "players' guide." If you're a player or a player wannabe, then put this book back on the shelf and go to the website of one of the leading men's magazines and get one of those "how to pick up women" books or whatever. But that is not this book's purpose. This is a handbook for that well-meaning American "good guy" who might even be a successful dater, but somehow doesn't quite know how to seal the deal with respect to achieving the next step with women. And by the "next step" I mean a meaningful relationship, not just a roll in the hay. Women are one of God's greatest creations, and it is a wise and fortunate man who knows how to totally interact with such precious examples of humanity.

This is a book based on real life experiences of the author over the course of a decade of activity on the dating scene, and while those experiences are my own, the lessons taught herein are timeless. At least two women (successful and professional in their own right), back then, suggested that I write such a book, as in their minds, the way I had treated them was the way they had always wanted to be treated by men. They also mentioned that they'd like something published to give their own sons to mitigate their making the same mistakes that men had made in dealing with them. Mind you, these suggestions had been made in both instances after we had split up, so

I like to think that I did something right.

While the experiences that led to the writing of this book are those of an educated professional in the Washington, D.C. area, I would like to think that they are universal and, with some variation for regional or local differences, the lessons learned from them can be applied anywhere. While the reader, who may not be as far along in his professional career, may find that his budget doesn't afford him the luxury of pursuing some of the suggestions contained in this book, a serious application of imagination will assist him in getting the most out of what his pocketbook will allow. However, this book is designed for the successful professional male who likes the finer things in life and is looking for a long-term relationship with a lady with whom to share that life.

This is a book on assisting the American male to develop healthy and meaningful heterosexual relationships. The author has no experience with the other kind and doesn't feel qualified in offering suggestions in that realm. Pick another tome for help in that area.

With these qualifications in mind, happy reading and good luck in finding a meaningful relationship with a wonderful – and lucky – lady. The author would love to receive feedback on what techniques offered herein worked for you – and which didn't.

Finally, this book is not an instruction on determining whether, once you have achieved a meaningful relationship, you should get married. Such a decision is too personal and determinant on too many factors unique to the two of you to be reduced to a handbook. Be mindful that many successful long-term relationships (Goldie Hawn and Kirk Russell and Gene Simmons and Shannon Tweed to name but two examples) exist where the couple has decided not to get married. So, once having achieved happiness together, whether you subsequently adorn it with a ring on her finger is up to you two. Good luck!

Table of Contents

Chapter One
Getting Yourself Ready

"The meeting of two personalities is like the contact of two chemical substances: if there is any reaction, both are transformed."

Carl Jung

Y ou wouldn't think of going to a job interview without being the most presentable you could be, would you? Nor would you try to run a competitive race without being ready for it, now would you? So why put yourself out on the dating market unless you were in the most tip-top "shape" you could? Sure, you might luck into a relationship with someone with low expectations, but then later when you're back on top of your game, you're with someone with either low self esteem or is someone with whom you don't really relate. By in "shape," I'm not just talking about physical shape. But to meet and have a chance to develop a meaningful relationship with quality women, you must bring your "A game" to the table. When I was ready, I held an elective office in my home town, had been appointed to a high level office in the national government, and owned a home in one of the most prestigious neighborhoods in my town.

1

The reason why many people – men and women – these days find themselves still single well into their late-thirties or even forties is they are so into their careers. They are so all-consumed with making it in the professional world that everything else is secondary. They often have a great amount of business travel, they work weekends, they bring work home every night, and they barely have enough time to attend to their own personal needs, nevertheless have a meaningful relationship. Oftentimes they have "hook up buddies" (sometimes called "friends with benefits") that help them take care of nature's urgings, but this is no substitute for the real thing – a meaningful relationship.

So, one of the first things you need to do to get yourself into "shape" is to ask yourself, "Am I willing to do what it takes to have a meaningful relationship?" The answer might very well be "no." Now, that is not an indictment, nor necessarily a bad thing, but you must be honest with yourself. If making partner – or becoming the new regional sales manager – or whatever, is the most all-consuming thing in your life for the next "x" number of years, then so be it. You have made a decision that at least for the near-future, is what is most important in your life and that is what you will devote the bulk of your energies toward achieving. But if that is the case, then you are not in "shape" to be open to building a meaningful relationship.

I have met a number of young millionaires who are lonely as hell – for a reason. They consume so much of their waking day into building a business (and parenthetically making a lot of money) that they have no time for a relationship. When they do come across a quality woman, they are so linearly-focused that they are usually a bore and nothing comes of the encounter. When they do reach out, they have such a single dimension to their personal lives that unless the woman is out for money, there is nothing of value to offer a high quality gal. Obviously there are exceptions, but this is often the norm.

A second way of getting in "shape" involves your own personality. Often younger people who have not yet matured their thinking or their personality much beyond where they were in high school are neurotic messes. They think that all they need to be "complete" is to have a partner of the opposite sex with whom to share their lives and everything will "fall into place." Well, it doesn't work that way, pal. You need to get it together first. Develop your own personality first. Make yourself an interesting companion. Be someone who knows who he is, is comfortable with himself (accepting his own "warts" because, let's face it, we all have them), cares about others, and is willing to open himself up to others. One of the things about clichés is they got that way because they are often oh so true, and one of the clichés that applies here is that if you're not willing to open your heart, it's doubtful if someone else will open up theirs to you. But you, my friend, are responsible for your own happiness – no one else. You need to be happy with yourself, first. Then, the odds of your being able to make someone else happy go way up.

We all know guys who, five or ten years after college, have the exact same lifestyle as they did back in school. Sure they work hard, but then they're usually in some bar after work drinking themselves silly; then they go back to their pig sty of an apartment and crash on the couch until it's time to get up and go back to work in the morning. One or two evenings a week is taken up with either a company softball team or a rec league basketball game; other than that, nothing changes. Unless they hook up with an old college girlfriend or meet someone in a bar with whom they click, they are likely to retain the same lifestyle for years. What a waste. They are not getting themselves in "shape." They need to work on themselves. There are two old adages that apply: one is that you are in ten years what you're reading now; the other is who you are is determined by whom (the type of people, not necessarily the individuals) you hang out with.

What to do? Examine yourself. Would *you* (be honest) go out with yourself? If you were going to fix up your sister, would you really fix her up with someone like yourself? If not, why not? If not, sit down and draw up a plan to get yourself in "shape." Cover all aspects of your personal life: your personality, your manners, your education, your body, your "interesting factor," your outlook, your ambitions, and your faith. Let's take them one at a time.

Personality

I've read medical reports concluding that a person's personality is set for life by the time that person was two. My response to that is "yes, but." I agree that if someone is basically an introvert, no amount of self-teaching or motivational lessons is going to convert them into the life of the party. However, one can be highly conscious of what one's basic personality is and then highlight or emphasize the positive points and downplay the not-so-positive points. If you are relatively successful in your professional life, then obviously you are already doing this to some extent. But when it comes to a meaningful one-on-one relationship with the opposite sex this becomes ever more difficult (in terms of hiding or "shading" the negative parts of one's personality) to do, and most people believe that even if someone were "putting on an act" to get someone to fall in love with them, that such acts expire after two years. The "real" self emerges in two years, and many relationships – married or not – terminate once the players revert to their real true selves and the partners realize that they made a mistake. So, I am not suggesting that you put on an act or hide anything about yourself. What I am suggesting is that you be overly-conscious of negative aspects of your personality and go out of your way to work on them. As a personal example, I have always been blessed with an excellent grasp of proper English grammar but cursed with an inability to let grammar errors of others go uncommented on. I know it's irritating to others to have me correct their grammar, especially those I love, so I have to consciously "turn off my editor" so as not to irritate those around me.

One good way to examine yourself, if you are not too thin skinned and are otherwise comfortable in that skin, is to invite three or four platonic women friends over for a glass of wine and ask them forthrightly what it is about your personality that they like and what they think you can improve upon. Don't get defensive about what you hear and try to keep your desire to respond to everything to a minimum, but take notes. You'll be surprised at what comes out. What you write down will be a good road map to follow to get on the right track.

When all else is said and done, survey after survey of American women have two qualities right up at the top which they say their ideal man must have: honesty and a sense of humor. The first is essential for any relationship; the second can almost guarantee a successful one. I would add a third attribute to honesty and humor – being non-judgmental. It is only natural for someone intelligent and "on-top-of-one's game" to have judgments about others, but for God's sake keep them to yourself. Voicing complaints or condemnations about things and people you see all day long (especially to your partner) makes you come across as a real ass; certainly as a requited cynic. Again, most people make mental judgments about others, just don't voice yours.

Manners

Most of us who were raised properly don't have much of a need for improvement in this area, but other than one's spoken words, nothing separates the differences in our society more than simple table manners – and manners in general. Wouldn't you feel terrible if you were to learn after your break up with the girl of your dreams that the real reason she never took you home to meet mommy and daddy was because she was afraid you'd embarrass her with your poor table manners? There are many books on the subject; go to the library, check one out, and *read* it. No library card? That alone says worlds about you and what you need to work on.

Education

Did you finish your degree? No, then good for you if you have a demanding, interesting, and hopefully rewarding job without it. But if not, why not? A degree is not just a "ticket" to financial success. It is an entry into the world of educated people; the cast of characters who actually run the world (and our governments at all levels, businesses, etc.). Many millionaires do not have a degree (Bill Gates anyone?), but unless you are already so smart and insightful that you've already found that niche, as did Gates to make his fortune, you should play the percentages and get one. A wise boss once told me that a man with a degree told a lot of positive things about himself: it meant that he had the drive and motivation to accomplish something that still only about 20% of the people in our country obtain. They see things through to fruition.

Already have a degree? What about a Masters? In Washington,

D.C. a Masters degree is the equivalent of a Bachelor's degree in most other cities. Look at the communities with the highest high school SAT scores. What do they have in common? A predominance of graduate degrees among the parents. You can take just one or two courses at a time at night in most cities while you continue in your day job. I used to say to people that I only got two things out of night graduate school: my wife and my job (true story). I just might add that in the context of this book, in graduate school, you meet a higher caliber woman! Just an added plus.

Body

Now you are going to come across those women, even higher-caliber women, who won't give you the time of day unless you're a 6'2" Adonis with abs of steel. You gotta read another book to reach those gals, as I don't know how to relate. Although I was an athlete in college and started out in a physically demanding profession (navy pilot), I've always had a bit of a weight problem. And I've run across women who were totally intrigued with my mind and personality, but it never crossed over into anything physical because I wasn't the Adonis-type. No matter; I wouldn't trade my life or the wonderful relationships I've had for anything. Women who were so shallow that they couldn't see beyond the fact that I was a little pudgy, weren't worth spending time with anyway. Heck, I'm a great guy! My own parents one time asked why I didn't lose twenty pounds so I could get a new wife, and I just responded that what women of quality were looking for was "just a nice guy."

But don't neglect the body. Number one, take vitamins. Usually a multi-vitamin, but often more. Vitamin C, especially during cold and flu season. Echinacea with Vitamin C, at the first sign of a scratchy throat or sniffles will oftentimes keep you from getting a cold; even if you do get one, the symptoms will be greatly reduced. I recently saw a brain surgeon on television describing cross sections of elderly peoples' brains on which he had operated. Other than Alzheimer's, the major difference he saw was that the healthier brains were patients who had taken Ginkgo Biloba. So, guess what I now take twice a day?

Join the gym or a health club. If you play racket sports, do that.

Many times I had a 7 a.m. squash match before the start of a demanding day. Somehow that got me more charged up than an after-work workout. A ski machine in my bedroom kept my cardiovascular system healthy for over ten years until I broke it. Now a treadmill does the trick. I don't subscribe to running outside; a colleague of mine was literally hit by a truck while running one morning during a business trip. Tends to ruin your whole day.

Golf is not only great exercise for bodies past the age of forty, but you can literally play it until your nineties. The fact that a great deal of business takes place on the golf course and more and more high quality women are taking up the game just add to its allure.

Are you a smoker? If so, ask yourself the question, have you ever kissed an ashtray? Well, my friend, that's what you'll taste like to any lady you kiss. Do you think that's a positive attribute? I don't think so. Now, in my past I smoked a pipe for thirteen years back in the era where it was more widely accepted (I once worked for an organization where almost every man and literally a couple of the women smoked pipes). I also occasionally smoke a good quality cigar, but I only do it by myself (or occasionally with a guy friend) and never in my own house. When I smoked, I always carried an aerosol breath spray or those breath sheets. Nothing's a worse turn off than to have smoke breath, and if you're an inveterate cigarette smoker, such breath aids will not cover up the fact. Besides, you're intelligent enough to know that you're most assuredly shortening your life. As an illustration, although my folks were in their eighties *every* one of their contemporaries who had smoked passed away in their seventies.

Check your hygiene. Does your breath smell? Besides having your teeth checked twice a year, brush and floss regularly. Carry a package of those little dissolvable breath strips – and use them. If your breath doesn't smell fresh, who in the world would want to kiss you? Come on, you're not a king; no one *has* to be attracted to you. You should eliminate all personal distractions that might otherwise detract a woman from wanting to get close to you (hair in your nose or ears, acne, body smell, etc.). Do your feet smell? If they do, that is an immediate and total turn off to a lady. It could be a sign that you have some other sort of health problem which a visit to a podiatrist can easily fix.

Another aspect of your "body" is how your appearance comes across. You may have toned your body to Olympian proportions, but if you've draped it shabbily you won't come across as looking your best. Prior to your beginning to look for a serious relationship, take a jaundiced look at your wardrobe. Is it as sharp as it could be? A wise friend once told me when I was in my first professional position that he couldn't afford designer or top-of-the-line suits, but he was able to get away with it by wearing top notch dress shirts and ties. Spend more than the average guy does on his ties and you'll look more successful than you are. Another friend told me about her girlfriend who lived in London. She only had one good outfit that she wore just when she traveled to Paris on business. Because of that expensive getup she was able to attract the eye of a rich duke who struck up a conversation. She ended up marrying royalty and now lives in estates in the English countryside and the Portuguese coast as a result.

"Interesting Factor"

There is another form of "education" with which you should become familiar in order to increase your "interesting factor." More properly the word is being well-read. Start off with the daily newspaper. Nothing is more vacuous to an educated person than to discover that her companion has no clue about what is going on in the world. Ditch diggers and other necessary but dead end job-holders fall into this category, so climb above that! If you don't subscribe to the newspaper but have the time and availability, go online daily to peruse the major occurrences in the world, in the nation, and in your community. You don't have to be a know-it-all, nor certainly an expert in any of it, but an aware, educated person is at least cognizant of what's going on around them. If you missed hearing of a story, just say, "Sorry, I missed that. Tell me about it." And genuinely listen to the story being related. The important thing is to be able to put it into context about what else is happening. There are certain internet sites (the Grudge Report is one of my favorites) that even contain links to the most widely published columnists nationwide. You don't have to agree or disagree with anything contained on such sites; the key is to know where to take the pulse quickly, so even if you just have five minutes during the day you can be caught up on key new developments. Or else you come across as that nerd who's been locked up in the basement of the science building!

The other "education" is reading. You should be reading something every day – even if it's just two paragraphs that put you to sleep every night. Your bedside stand should have two or three books that you are in the midst of reading. Either buy or check out of the library a best-selling novel once in awhile. Remember, you're trying to increase your "interesting factor" so that you're not just another slug with a nice smile and good hair – not that the latter is really important. The more you've read, the more interesting you are. At a dinner or cocktail party, you'll rarely be searching for a topic to discuss if you're well read. Just don't take it too far and become (in your own mind) the world's foremost authority on the subject you just read (remember, there are people around who have gotten PhD's on the subject about which you just read 300 pages).

It also helps to read something in addition to what everyone else is reading. So while others are parroting to each other the words on the front page story in your city's major paper you can be chiming in with the take of some other periodical or journalist on the same topic. I had a well-meaning friend once describe me as her "resident scholar" just because I'd read a couple of books on the topic being discussed. I claim in no way to be a scholar, but I'd like to say I'm fairly well-read – and interesting.

Outlook

Nothing is more of a turn off – to men or women – than hanging around a constantly negative person. They bring everyone else down. Now, you don't need to look at life with rose-colored glasses, but isn't it just as easy to see that the glass is half full as it may seem half empty? A genuinely positive outlook on life promotes optimism, hope, a zest for the future, and offers a potential life-time partner a real palpable hook on which to hang her hopes for the future. If you have a good attitude about yourself, you are more likely to also have a good outlook toward having a strong, healthy relationship with a high quality lady.

Ambitions

We've already touched on this in the opening paragraphs of this chapter. Suffice it to say that while over-ambition can be a serious roadblock toward achieving a meaningful relationship with a high quality woman, the lack of it may ensure that no spark even gets started. Most high quality women don't expect the man in their life to be worth tons of money, but neither do they want to have to support him. Neither do they demand that you be a professional. But they have a right to expect that whatever your chosen field, you have ambitions to succeed at it – be it a daycare provider or a rocket scientist. I have a good friend who's a professional woman from the Philippines and who would invite me to join her and her American husband at Philippine cultural events. The group was replete with women physicians married to hard-working and successful blue collar workers.

Faith

Faith is tricky. Oftentimes, two people strike up a relationship that is purely intellectual, emotional, and physical. What else is there, you might ask? The answer is faith. In the modern world, our society often seems split between the 50% who are avid church goers and most of the remainder who don't give it a second thought – who literally never think about who they are, why they are here, how they got here, or what's next after they leave here. I submit that if you're going to have a *meaningful* relationship with a woman of the modern era, then you're going to have had a few conversations on this topic before the relationship develops too far. There really is no right or wrong belief (when you delve into the basic tenets of each, the core teachings of Christianity, Judaism, Islam, and Buddhism are quite similar – don't know much about the rest), but your quality lady is going to expect that you believe in something. Remember that old adage: if you don't stand for something, then you'll fall for anything? There's something to it. I'm not suggesting that you enter into impassioned religious debates with someone you've just started dating. But you really ought to examine beforehand what you believe and why and be ready to discuss it intelligently with someone you care about. You should also have in mind what beliefs you can accept and what you cannot (Satanism, animal sacrifice – one never knows!). It doesn't mean you have to accept or practice what she does, but a stronger bond usually develops between people who share somewhat the same view of a Supreme Being. A belief in some form of the Almighty can successfully bring your relationship through truly hard times that a bond between two people with split beliefs might not.

As a footnote to this chapter, we need to address the very real question of whether you're really in "shape" to seek out another meaningful relationship if you've recently just terminated an existing one – whether it be a divorce, former live-in girlfriend, or what have you. A wise friend once told me that he never dated a woman unless she'd been divorced for at least two years. I ignored him and proceeded to be the "rebound relationship" for at least a half-dozen wonderful ladies who had just ended their marriages. In retrospect, I wished I'd listen to my friend. The same could very well go for you. If nothing else, it will take awhile to get references to your former spouse/partner out of your patter, and I remember being told by several ladies that I seemed to still have a thing for my wife (quite untrue, by the way). It's just that she was a high quality person, she was the mother of my children, and she had been the central focus of my personal life for over 15 years, so what was wrong with that? What was wrong was that my dates didn't want to hear it, and they quite properly wondered if I was really ready to focus on them. After two years or so, I guess I finally was.

Chapter Two
Where to Meet Ms. Right

"Sometimes when you look back on a situation, you realize it wasn't all you thought it was. A beautiful girl walked into your life. You fell in love. Or did you? Maybe it was only a childish infatuation, or maybe just a brief moment of vanity."

Henry Bromel, *Northern Exposure*, The Big Kiss, 1991

The most obvious place to meet the woman of your dreams might seem too obvious – work. But be very, very careful, especially if you are in a managerial or leadership position. Then you must be very discrete, and your actions must be correct in every sense of the word – or you could get fired or worse (disregard this if you're a Member of Congress, since you and your colleagues have chosen to exempt yourself from the every day statutes that guide the rest of us mere mortals). If the woman in question is more than a few years younger than you, be doubly careful. A man in a position of authority who asks a sweet young thing to lunch is playing with fire. The female in question might really have an interest in your entreaties; however, you won't know until after you've received the face-to-face briefing by the head of HR (with the attendant note in your personnel file) that the young lady felt intimidated by the invitation and accepted only because she thought a declination would adversely affect her career with the organization. Having said that, if she is a colleague at your level in the organization (especially if functionally your paths never cross), have at it.

I mean, er, ah....by all means ask her to lunch. If she says "no," then take it to heart (but not personal) and move on. If she says "no," but has a valid excuse (not, she has to organize her pencils) then ask her again. But the key is to be friendly, not intimidating and certainly not creepy. Keep it light and friendly at lunch, too. As soon as you can, if it appears that you are indeed attracted to her, get the conversation off business and onto her. Again, don't pay creepy attention; just ask about her and find out who she is and what her interests are. Take her to nothing more formal than a deli, a pizza joint, or a small family-owned place. Nothing fancier than a Chinese food place, but not if the seating is nothing more than chairs for carry out customers.

Company softball teams are fruitful areas to explore in terms of developing relationships with quality women at work. However, even if something does develop you must be extremely careful about being discrete, especially if out-of-town travel entails opportunities to be with her. Failure to do so can affect both of your personal and professional reputations. While work offers a fruitful field of potential lifetime partners, it also entails additional challenges to ensure that reputations don't suffer in the process from the inevitable gossip and backstabbing that goes on. The obvious downside to dating someone from work is: what is going to happen if the relationship goes somewhere but doesn't become permanent? Then tremendous problems can ensue after the break up if you still have to work together on a daily basis. In fact it can affect both your performances and potentially both your careers.

On the other hand, what if it does become permanent? Some organizations have policies precluding members of the same family from working together or even from both being employed. Especially if one of the two partners is at the head of the unit in which you are employed, one of you may have to find employment elsewhere. All this involves a mature evaluation before one lets oneself become entailed in a relationship at work.

So, other than work, where does one find quality women these days? Television would have you believe that the gym/spa is a fruitful place to do so. However, it has been my experience that people seriously involved in toning their bodies or getting exercise, completely separate the strictly physical element of their beings from the emotional side. So unless you just happen to be lucky enough to encounter a "Miranda Hobbs" walking to her car after her daily morning workout, chances are you'll find better pickings elsewhere. Not that fantastic women aren't found at the gym; it's just that it's rare that their antenna are out for that purpose at the spa.

Evening classes, as was mentioned in the last chapter, are a good place to meet quality women. Often after class, a few folks will gather at a nearby watering hole to kick around the latest assignment or topic of study. Numerous relationships have developed in such settings, and potential partners can explore relatively risk-free each other's intellectual capacities without it being some sort of competition. Any type of class, now that I think of it (except for Lamaze classes obviously), is a good place to meet high quality women. Additionally, you are learning a skill or talent that will assist in making you a more "interesting" person. Dog obedience classes, cooking classes, investment classes, self-help classes, photography classes, and foreign language classes are all examples that afford opportunities to meet great ladies. Certain types of clubs also fit the bill, especially book, investment, and travel clubs. Take a dance studio class for lessons in ballroom dancing, fox trot, or whatever dance is popular. The majority of my educated single women friends like guys who can and will dance. If a guy is a great dancer, he earns an automatic plus on a woman's checklist of things she wants to find in a guy.

Church activities are an obvious choice to meet women of quality. Personally, I never had much success at the church-sponsored singles activities, but a diverse and active congregation presents numerous functions at which people from all aspects of the community come together, formally and informally. Discussion groups provide opportunities to watch others lead in devotional and even business conversations. One must be careful to not appear to be "trolling for dates", but opportunities do present themselves.

A great way to meet incredible ladies is to join a choral group.

Such organizations range from church choirs, to informal madrigal ensembles, to community choirs, to the Mormon Tabernacle Choir. The more formal the group, the more time commitment they require, so be cognizant of that. Church choirs usually require attendance at Wednesday or Thursday night rehearsals as well as early Sunday morning rehearsal prior to commencement of services. The more formal groups (e.g., the Sweet Adeline's/Barbershop Quartets) offer out-of-town and even foreign travel to participate in performances and competitions. There are usually a few unattached and incredible ladies who are members of such groups. The downside, again, is the awkwardness that will surround your being part of a closely-knit group containing someone with whom a relationship did not work. If you can't sing, learn how to play an instrument. Every decent sized metropolitan area has a symphony, and playing first-rate music with other amateurs can offer hours of pleasurable entertainment and diversion – even if you don't find the "one for you" amidst other band members.

Believe it or not, the library is a fruitful area to meet women of quality. Often I used to visit the periodical section so as to obviate my house from being filled with too many magazines. Evenings and rainy weekends presented outstanding times to find the library teeming with educated single women. Again, care must be taken so as not to appear creepy, and it is hard to appear friendly in a library without appearing creepy so you must work at it to get your approach right. Rare was the rainy weekend, especially if there were a football game on, that I didn't visit both the library and the grocery store. Now I like football as much as the next guy, but unless it's the Super Bowl, the world is not going to come to an end if you miss part of the game. So the people you find out and about at those times are women, guys! Grocery stores in or near affluent urban neighborhoods on Saturday mornings are replete with opportunities to develop your social skills and to learn what the single woman of today likes to eat. Grocery stores within five miles of major airports often are filled on Saturdays with flight attendants stocking up for the weekend, since they have been elsewhere during the week.

Wine tastings are probably the one example that I have found where high quality women attend in pairs, and better yet, they are in a semi-partying mood. Now true wine tastings are not held so the patrons can guzzle copious amounts of wine, but such events hosted by reputable wine stores usually entail 20-40 people sipping an ounce or two of a couple dozen wines over a two hour period. At such events, there is ample opportunity to meet and become acquainted with high quality ladies who share your love of the mighty grape (more about that later)! In addition to such wine tastings, there are wine clubs that meet in restaurants. While these entail a greater expense, as a meal usually attends the tasting, they not only increase your education about the fruit of the vine, they are also attended by a great many quality women. Even better are wine tasting courses offered by many fine wine stores. Seeing the same people week after week for a couple of months enables you to get to know the participants in depth, and who knows?

Art galleries are other places to meet women of quality. You already share a refined interest, and if you bump into someone while admiring the same painting, what more introduction do you need?

If you're a single parent, after school day care is a great place to meet single mothers. Usually it takes several months of seeing the same parents picking up their darlings before you ferret out who's single and who's "available," but once you do one hurdle is obviously past: you have established that you have similar interests. While I have little experience attending PTA meetings (I was usually attending to other municipal business while PTA meetings were occurring), it seems to me that they offer another opportunity to meet and become acquainted with single mothers.

Meeting ladies on the subway or buses is not recommended. After all, how can even a discerning woman differentiate between you and the real serial killer standing next to you? Now, if you happen to see the same woman week after week after week, and she seems like a high quality lady, offer a casual "hi" on occasion. If it's returned with anything zestier than an "hmph" then perhaps an opportunity has presented itself.

Charity and political events are great opportunities to meet high quality women. The added attraction of doing something good for your community or the party you believe in is only enhanced by the possibility of meeting smart and committed women who very likely might share your outlook on life.

What is missing from the foregoing discussion? That's right, bars! If you're looking for a quick score, great! But I have yet to meet a woman of high quality at a bar with whom I would consider having a meaningful relationship. Now I know that is a gross generalization – and there are exceptions such as business and political conventions and post-softball game gatherings – but I have found it rare that successful women hang out together in bars. Remember, if you want to know what your life will be like in ten years, examine who you're hanging out with.

Lastly, a discussion about the two sources of hook ups of the modern age: the Internet and the personal ads. First, the personal ads.

I'm a great believer in percentages. If you want to make admiral, you go to the Naval Academy, right? That's just playing the percentages. So, if you want to meet the right woman, why not maximize your chances by advertising for same. Why not, I did. Almost every major metropolitan newspaper and most similar city-related magazines have personal columns. Add to that the internet sites such as Craig's List, and even Yahoo, and you have quite an array of advertising venues from which to choose. Both personal ads and Internet dating services both wisely advise women to be smart and play it safe in the location and circumstances of where and how they first meet guys from both sources. For different reasons, I would advise that you do the same.

Your ad should show a sense of humor and a capacity to not take yourself too seriously. It should above all be honest. The one thing most people lie about is their weight. In answering ads or receiving responses to my ad from women of "medium build" I have encountered ladies weighing from 120 to 250 pounds. Go figure. It's a crap shoot, what can I tell you? But don't play that game. If you have an Ivy League education, say it. If you don't, so what, but don't claim to have one. Is it worth having a falsehood attract a lady to want to go on a date, only to have it later blow up in your face once it comes out that you made it up? I don't think so. Women of quality don't expect you to be a physician with a trust fund. They want someone who's honest, not too stuck on themselves, and stable – emotionally and financially. In short, someone with whom they can build a future.

Keep your ad relatively short and punchy and use levity where you can. Include your interests and the traits you're looking for.

Stress the latter more than the former; who you are and what you like to do will come out in the first contact. If the personal ad system involves giving you a chance to leave a voice message on a phone answering system, great. Write your script out ahead of time and don't be afraid to edit it if it's not perfect the first time. Keep a smile in your voice and keep it light. No woman wants to hear a Darth Vader type-voice intoning about how you're going to turn her world upside down. Include a thanks for responding to your ad and say you're looking forward to meeting with her if she thinks she'd be interested in doing so.

As for the Internet, I highly recommend it. I met my second wife on the Internet, no kidding. But this was after five years of meeting the wrong people. I take that back, I met one charming lady; she just happened to be just geographically undesirable (four hours away). The best sites are ones that allow you to film a small interview of yourself and/or that permit you to make your own choices of whom you want to meet. I once tried a computer dating service that provided you with one name at a time based on a "match" of the qualities you enunciated. After two years of using them, the only thing I could tell they were matching was age. Nothing else correlated, and it cost a lot of money.

Unless you are underemployed (or independently wealthy), the only way to proceed once you have your personal ad in or have made your selection off the Internet is to be selective. Examine each candidate comprehensively with respect to mutuality of interests, not with whom you think you can most easily score. Narrow it down to half a dozen and in no fixed order call one and schedule a time and place to meet somewhere for a cup of coffee. Starbucks is a perfect venue for meeting such a person. It's public; it's usually pretty busy; there's usually a place to sit; many are adjacent to book stores (yay!); and you're out less than ten bucks if things don't click between you two. If there's no Starbucks handy, the major book stores these days have their own coffee shops (I first met my second wife at a Border's Books coffee shop after we were introduced and communicated online). While they're public, they're not too noisy; yet, no one minds if you have a conversation. And if you two really don't click, you have all these great books to peruse afterwards.

Chapter Three
The First Introductory Meeting

"Love is the delightful interval between meeting a beautiful girl and discovering that she looks like a haddock."

John Barrymore

Okay, the contact has been made and you've obtained her phone number. Now what? There is no hard and fast rule about when you should actually call the lady. Hollywood has written many scripts about the "two day" rule; most involve some sort of role playing or posturing. A lot of that is hooey. There's no hard and fast rule. If you're really swamped with work; you're really swamped at work. However, if she makes a big thing of it about *really* calling her when she gives you the number, then be gentlemanly and call her within the next two to four days. Sure it might be that she's desperate, but did you ever stop to think that it's because she is generally attracted to you?

The first call shouldn't be made when you're rushed or when you're amidst a crowd of people. Generally, she's going to give you a cell number (many folks these days don't even have a land line). So, the first thing to say when she answers the phone is to tell her who you are (don't be a conceited ass and assume) and ask her if it's a good time for her to chat. If she doesn't remember who you are then she's either playing a game to get "one up" on you, or she's a player and she's got so many dudes calling her that it's not worth your while. Sure, she might be a great lady but remember, you've now gotten yourself in "shape," you're ready with your "A game" and you don't need some distaff player doing what you used to do. Have an airy chat, say "see ya'," and look elsewhere. Also, the first contact should not be an email or text message. Those are for when you're already more familiar with each other and can have a casual chat.

Assuming that the initial phone call goes well, suggest that the two of you meet for a cup of coffee as discussed in the last chapter. Only if she insists, an alternative would be to meet somewhere for a glass of wine. Don't put too much emphasis on getting together, but stress either that you were attracted to her or thought that she seemed interesting and you wanted to get to know her better and set it up.

The one complaint that I continually hear from many of my lady friends about their first meeting with a guy is the guy talks incessantly about himself. Hey, gents, this isn't an interview to get into college or to obtain a job; it's a dialogue to establish if there's any mutual interest in really getting to know this person. Why is her getting to know you any more important than you getting to know her? You should care a lot more about her than the fact that she has breasts and a vagina (and if you are still *too* focused on that stuff then you have a lot more growing up to do than she – or I – can help you with).

Most likely, she did better than you in school and often has a more demanding or a more prestigious (whatever that means) job. Don't make her regret that she decided to meet you. Remember the "interesting factor" we talked about in the first chapter? Hopefully, you can hold up your end of the conversation, but even if you've been literally buried in nothing but work related crap for the past week, you'll do fine if you show a genuine interest in finding out who she is and what she's all about.

Any decent conversation, whether at work or in these situations, is like climbing a ladder together. You each have to meet each other on every "floor" for it to work. While you should offer up bits of information about yourself to match what she's sharing, watch out for the "one-upsmanship" syndrome. That's when, no matter what story she has to offer about a particular situation, say it's something as mundane as dealing with her organization's mailroom, you have a better story on the same point. That's not cool.

Anyway, it's always best to schedule such meetings after work or in the early or mid-afternoon on weekends, so that you can gracefully wrap it up after no more than two or three hours and each go on your way. If you're still interested after what you've learned of and about her, just tell her that the meeting has been fun and ask if she'd like to go to dinner sometime. Again, you're not asking her to marry you – just share a meal.

It's either yes, no, or let me check with my calendar. If she's carrying a Blackberry then stand there and let her check it; if she refrains, sorry pal, no sale. Don't worry, you still have other irons in the fire, right?

If you decide to ask one of these incredible ladies on a formal first date, do yourself a favor. Call her to ask. Never use email or a text message for a first date invitation. While it may seem to you an expedient and quick method, to her it seems that you're either too chicken to speak with her directly or too lazy to ask her out properly. Any woman who receives a first date invitation electronically (other than the telephone) is totally within her rights to blow you off and forget about you forever. So, don't get sloppy. Keep emails and texts to when you already have something going with a woman and the informality has been earned.

Chapter Four
The First Date

"Oh, the comfort - the inexpressible comfort of feeling safe with a person - having neither to weigh thoughts nor measure words, but pouring them all right out, just as they are, chaff and grain together; certain that a faithful hand will take and sift them, keep what is worth keeping, and then with the breath of kindness blow the rest away."

~Dinah Craik, *A Life for a Life*, 1859

On the first date with a woman, I always presented them with a single long-stem red rose. These days every grocery store has a floral department, and even if no one's manning the shop, you can pick out your own rose and maybe a sprig of baby's breath. Convenience stores have begun carrying a single flower, not always a rose, but I think they're too plasticized (some are literally in a plastic vial). Anyway, the flower's a nice touch. Never chocolate on the first date. The rose connotes that you think she might be special and you've taken the time to pick up something beautiful to leave with her to remind her that you think she just might be. Some people may find this practice "hokey" but let them think so. It separates you from the pack. It shows you have style.

When you pick her up, allow a couple of minutes for her to find a vase or something to put the flower in some water before you go sprinting off together. One time, I had a date with a beautiful FBI agent. It was a blind date and the friend setting me up told me what a fabulous sense of humor she had, so I showed up with a rose in one hand and a rubber chicken in the other. It sounded like a good idea at the time.

Usually I preferred that the first date with someone be a meal. Why? Because the whole venue is conducive to talking with and getting to know each other. This usually entails a dinner, but a favorite of mine was also the Sunday brunch at a nice hotel. Just be careful with those, as often they come with free champagne, which can result in either your sleeping the rest of the day or an ill-timed and premature roll in the hay on your first date. While that may seem desirable, I've occasionally had a promising relationship terminated rather early because the lady was tired of having a series of sexual relationships and was hoping to develop a longer term one based on friendship, mutual respect, and trust. Not that one of those can't develop from one that begins with sex on the first date, but that's not how these ladies wanted to proceed, and because they'd let their guard down too early due to the champagne, they ended it to begin differently with someone else in a non-sexual way.

Back to the dinner. At "first meals" always pull your date's chair out for them, even if you have to use considerable body language to the host/hostess who these days often steals the man's thunder and performs that function for the women when you have a party of two. Set the stage early that you are not only a nice guy, but you're well-mannered. If it's a small table, sit across from her; anything bigger and sit as close to her as possible – even if the table is set with the place setting across from her. This maximizes the opportunity to "connect" with each other. If the first table they lead you to is too public or is in the middle of the traffic pattern, and the restaurant is not totally full, politely ask if you might be shown a quieter table.

Ask the lady if she'd like a cocktail or would she prefer to share a bottle of wine. Most people prefer the latter unless they are inveterate martini drinkers. Ask her if she'd prefer red or white. Only if she insists on a white, get one of those – usually a mid-priced California Chardonnay (see recommended list in the Wine Appendix). Any other answer, order a red. Since Bordeaux and the best California Cabernet Sauvignon's are now so darn over-priced, aim for an Oregon Pinot Noir, a Syrah, or a red Zinfandel (never a white Zinfandel, yeeechh!). Careful with the Zin; the alcohol content can be 15 or 16% alcohol, and I have seen the attendees at a dinner with twenty people all get totally soused due to the high alcohol content. Once you have developed a meaningful relationship and you've learned the lady's palate, then by all means on special occasions order that special, higher-priced red wine. Better yet, call ahead to discern whether the restaurant permits you to bring your own wine and inquire as to the corkage fee for your waiter to open it. If no problem, then bring your own special bottle from your own "cellar," which need not be anything more than a simple closet.

Never order the meal for your date unless she invites you to do so, and trust me this is becoming even more a remote possibility as the years go by. Bright and capable women are as experienced trying new cuisines as are guys so they usually have their own opinions on what they'd like. If you happen to be at a restaurant of an ethnicity she's never before tried – or if you've been to that establishment before – then by all means make recommendations, but don't order for her unless she asks. It's being presumptuous on your part and connotes a controlling personality. It will immediately raise red flags with her. It does not show manliness; it shows callousness and conceit.

Unless you are under orders from your boss to always be available, turn your cell phone off during the meal. Nothing is more obnoxious to the other party nor as disconcerting in the middle of an intense or intimate conversation than to have a cell phone ring. Besides, it's rude to answer it in front of your date. Again, there are exceptions such as if you told your best friend or your roommate that you'd pick him up at the airport, so you left the phone on in case his flight arrived early.

You should leave the decision on whether to have dessert to your date. Many times she'll offer to split one, so agree readily. Similarly, the question of coffee or an after-dinner libation should be her choice.

I prefer a meal on such a first date as it really gives you both an opportunity to discuss things with each other. Leave religion or politics out of the conversation, though that's tough in a place like Washington, D.C. where politics is the topic du jour whether you're involved in that profession or not (sort of like the entertainment industry would be in LA or the high tech business would be in Silicone Valley). I once had a friend from New York say about DC: "people in this town only talk about three things: who won the latest primary, who won the latest election, or who's screwing whom." Discussion should start with the subject of what brought you together, i.e., the wine tasting, the library, the competency of the day care, or whatever. From that you could branch out to jobs, school, career, her family, her home town, and so on. Remember, climb the ladder with her. Canned jokes aren't really in order, but the ability to see levity in the general topic being discussed expresses your sense of humor and makes it known that you're a fun person to be with.

The duration of the dinner is flexible. Every conversation has its own edge and flow. If one or both of you is fatigued, either because of the demands of the day or the week, then wrap it up. If not, as long as you're fully engaged and there's not a long line with the attendant maitre d' tapping his foot at you, then don't wrap things up before you're ready.

If the conversation is still going long and strong, then by all means go for a short drive. If there's a safe and scenic place to park – and I'm not talking about a lover's lane – then stop there for awhile. Airports always have safe places nearby to park and watch the jets take off and land. There's something mesmerizing about these avionic evolutions. But this is suggested only if your date is one of those situations where it seems like you've known each other forever and the conversation is flowing unbelievably smoothly. If not, then call it a night and take her home.

The subject of the first date goodnight kiss has received almost as much play in the movies as the timing of the first phone call. My recommendation is that, assuming there is some sort of connection between you, either give her a quick peck on the lips or a long and warm hug. Thank her for a great evening and say you're looking forward to seeing her again. Long lip locks are the sign of either a "player" or someone who's desperate. Always leave her wanting more.

It is a good idea after a first date to, either late that night or early the next day, send her a text message to tell her how much you enjoyed the date and to say that you're looking forward to hanging out with her again. By texting her, it is an unobtrusive way to express this and is a nice touch that will be appreciated. You know that either that night or early the next morning, she's going to be on the horn to her closest friends telling them about how it went with "the new guy." So, don't call her until at least noon on the next day. Know for sure that some of what they'll be feeding her will be off-the-wall stuff, but by now she knows which of her friends have instincts she trusts, and usually she'll trust her own. Assuming you trust your own, and you still have a warm feeling about your time with her, then call her in the afternoon. Be friendly and keep it light. Repeat that you had a great time and listen to her response. Don't be so needy that you need her reinforcement by asking her if she did, too. She'll volunteer if she did. If she doesn't volunteer, that still doesn't mean that she didn't. She's just playing it close to the vest. She doesn't want to appear too eager. Hopefully before you call, you'll have an idea to suggest regarding your next outing.

Chapter Five
The Second Date

"All love that has not friendship for its base, is like a mansion built upon sand."

Ellen Wheeler Wilcox

When I have an especially good feeling about the way things went with the lady on the first date, I invite her to dinner at my house for our second date. In the winter, this is especially cool as you can sit on the couch in front of the fire place and finish the dinner wine and continue the conversation begun at the dinner table.

Now don't panic at the thought of having to cook dinner. You don't have to be a gourmet cook (but, again, taking a cooking course at the local community college is still another great way to meet women of quality), but it is even more fun – once a sound relationship has been established – to cook together on a Friday or Saturday night. My specialty is Spanish paella, and while it is a lot of work, it is delicious and a great hit either serving two on a weekend, on special occasions like a going away dinner for good friends, or for an intimate dinner for two on New Year's Eve (see Appendix Three for the recipe).

The meal should always be focused around the wine you're serving. I one time cooked a dinner for two other couples and my date built around six different wines. While I superbly matched the six courses around a half dozen fantastic bottles, I almost killed myself with the effort and I don't recommend it – until and unless you have a developed relationship so your date can help, in the serving if not also in the preparation.

For this second date, all you need is two medium-sized steaks, two baked potatoes (with sour cream and butter), two mixed salads (greens, carrettes, cherry tomatoes, and Italian dressing), and a great Cabernet Sauvignon. Open the wine an hour early to let it breathe, make the salads and leave them covered in the refrigerator so the greens don't wilt. Set the table – with candles. Pour the wine fifteen minutes before she arrives, at which time you poke holes in the potatoes with a fork and microwave them for 10 minutes. Throw the steaks on the broiler after seasoning them with Seasonall, and cook them four to five minutes per side (more if she likes hers well done). Warm the plates by sticking them in the microwave for 60 seconds after you've pulled the spuds out. Put dressing on the salads and put them on the table, seat her, and put her warm plate in front of her.

Dessert is in the 'fridge which you've made the night before: a yogurt pie. Buy a pre-cooked graham cracker crust pie shell. Mix in a bowl two containers of the same kind of fruit yogurt and a cup of Cool Whip; then dump it into the pie shell. Cool overnight in the refrigerator. Piece of cake!

Your dinner should be comfortable and easy. Your house/ apartment is picked up but not necessarily maid-clean. Don't worry about it – you're not a slob, but you're a guy. Trust me, she's going to be blown away at the quality of your wine, the fact that you didn't burn the dinner (you didn't did you??), the quality of the books on your shelves (ever been in a living room containing no books, kind of weird's you out doesn't it?), and the sparkling nature of your conversation. The pie is just the icing on the cake (oh, to mix those metaphors!).

After dinner, if she offers, let her help you clear the table but seriously, just stack them in the sink and clean them later. How anal are you? Grab her by the hand, pick up your glasses and what remains in the bottle, and head for the couch next to the fire place. If it's not winter and greater than 70 degrees out, sit outside (get some sort of love seat- sized swing; they're great!) Again, it's too early in this building-the-meaningful-relationship process to want or expect her to make love to you, nor should you really want to. Dude, you're still getting to know her! But nothing gives you as warm a feeling as that before the fire with a glass of wine in one hand and the other one on the end of an arm encircling a fascinating creature you're really getting to know. After an hour or so, get up to cut each of you a piece of pie and offer her coffee. After all, she *is* driving home later tonight.

What if she demurs about the idea of coming to your place on only the second date? Now, I've never had an offer to cook a lady dinner turned down but you never know. Even if she did come for dinner on the second date, the third date will suffice as the answer to the aforementioned question. So if she says "no" about coming over, hopefully by now, you know enough about each other that you have a little bit of an idea of her interests and where you could take her. Assuming she has not expressed a complete distaste for any of the following, I would suggest: a play (especially a community play in a smaller theater), miniature golf, roller skating, a trip to the zoo or a nature park, a winery tour, a bike ride, a picnic, a museum, an art gallery visit, or a boat ride.

Personally, I preferred either the first activity on the list or the last. Season tickets to the theater, the opera, the symphony, the ballet and/or all of the above are nice to have and offer many opportunities to take women of quality. Of course the timing of those events is pre-set and they might not coincide with your second or third date. But the benefits they offer are considerable for the larger dating picture: the longer you have them, the better seats you can get; you are assured of tickets to the shows of greatest demand; and you get to see some fantastic productions. A night at the theater doesn't necessarily involve dinner. Sometimes performances are on a weeknight, and there's no chance for one or both of you to get away from work sufficiently early to have a meal. If the event was at the Kennedy Center, I always took her to the rooftop restaurant for dessert and coffee or liqueur afterwards. This also serves to obviate your getting caught in the traffic crunch when leaving. A special treat is available if your locality has an outdoor venue. These usually offer the option of paying for seats under a roof or blanket space on the grass. Either way, it's usually a very fun event – and if you plan ahead and the weather cooperates you can eat a meal and share some wine on a blanket and then take your seats closer up under the roof to enjoy the performance.

As for the boat ride, nothing beats a nice boat (20 feet or larger) for a wonderful day with an incredible woman. Suggest that she pack a light lunch and inquire if she'd prefer wine, beer, or soda which you will provide (whatever she picks, be sure to also bring along a couple of bottles of spring water as being on a boat is dehydrating). Obviously, you are also providing the transportation to the vessel, the gas and other boating expenses, and the expertise for running the thing. Don't know anything about boating? The internet can direct you to a number of local schools and organizations that teach the why's and wherefore's of the activity. Remember the bit about being honest? It especially applies if you're contemplating taking the lady out on a boat. I've operated and owned boats (sail and power) my whole life, and the idiotic things that novices do on the water would curl your hair. If you really have a notion to take a woman on a boat and you do not know what you're doing, by all means ask a friend who has one to take you both out. It will likely save a possible disaster (and the attendant legal liability) and sure embarrassment if you do.

If the boat is close by (less than a half hour) you can literally do the whole date in three hours or less; however, if it is any farther away, it is an all-day evolution. So be sure you're really into her before you suggest an all-day event as a lack of shared-interests or incompatibility will come through loud and clear if you have to be in a car with someone for a combined total of two hours added to the one-to-four hours on the water. Another cautionary note about boating with complete novices: the first few times, never ask them to stand in the bow, dock line (it's *not* a rope!) in hand, and – as most experienced boaters do – leap aboard the pier or to be able to tie the line around the post, cleat, or piling. If there's someone on the pier ready to receive the line, OK, but absent that you rush forward to do it after you've put the boat in neutral (I know the preferred maneuver is to back her slightly after your first line is secure but you must compensate for your inexperienced crew). I have known guys who've had to console (and dry off) their dates who've misjudged the leap ashore or worse. Most folks don't bring along a replacement outfit, and no woman is going to feel completely comfortable after being immersed in her valiant effort to play bowman. So play it safe. While underway, unless they're experienced (or at least they've taken a course, perhaps the Coast Guard's excellent Power Squadron course), don't ask them to steer in congested places or where navigational or rules-of-the-road issues will come into immediate play. On the open water, by all means let them steer (if they're interested), and if they can drive a car, they can usually steer a boat if you indicate the point of land or compass direction at which you wish them to aim. However, a serious relationship of mine was almost seriously damaged when, despite such explicit directions on steering my sailboat, there was a most unfortunate collision between my head and the boom while I was altering the head sail, because she was too into enjoying the experience and had not paid sufficient attention to where she was steering. Enough said.

As with any event outdoors, for boating don't assume *anything* is known about the activity and gently suggest in detail the type of dress and accoutrements that should be brought (i.e., jackets, hats, rubber-soled shoes – preferably tennis shoes with white soles, sunscreen, sunglasses, etc.). As an example, one time this lady entreated me to take her to play squash and when I picked her up, I asked her where her gym shoes were. Her response was that I had mentioned she needed rubber-soled shoes and these were they. I fell on the floor laughing; her rubber-soled shoes were rubber-soled high-heeled sandals tied to her ankles with ribbons. With her tiny ankles she would have broken at least one of them and sprained the other inside of five minutes. We immediately ditched that idea and went to brunch instead.

Each type of vessel offers its own benefits. A power boat can allow you to go fast, cover a lot of territory, and water ski (if you're so inclined and have the gear and the skill, but keep in mind if it's only the two of you, it's likely that unless she's already proficient on the water, only she will go skiing). A sail boat offers a communing with nature that is rare in the modern world with only the sound of the wind and the waves to affect your senses (I usually only played either Beethoven or Buffet under sail). Five knots on a beam reach can seem to be as fast as going twenty knots in a power boat. You can fish off either type of vessel, but be sure the boat is properly licensed and that the license covers anyone aboard to fish without additional licensure (not to point out the obvious, but every state is different and the requirements do change). On neither type of vessel should *anyone* be permitted to become intoxicated; even good swimmers can succumb if the water is cold, the boat traffic heavy and/or the skipper is also bombed. It's just not smart. And nowhere else does it become so readily apparent that alcohol is indeed a depressant, not a stimulant. In hot, humid weather you may become extremely dehydrated after a couple of beers because your body needs fluids, not alcohol, and you soon have the scientific fact proved to you when your body completely craves pure water to replenish what the beers have caused to eek out of you.

If her delicious lunch didn't satiate, you can always stop for a quick burger or pizza on the way home (indeed, given the precarious nature of sailboats' delicate electrical systems, I have occasionally had to resort to enjoying the lady's picnic lunch on the grass next to the marina while the batteries were charging). At her door, why not a goodnight (or good day) kiss? Heck, you might have already stolen one as she sat next to you in the sailboat's cockpit (another benefit over a power boat, which usually has bucket seats for the driver).

Chapter Six
The Infamous Third Date

"When you give each other everything, it becomes an even trade. Each wins all."

Lois McMaster Bujold, *A Civil Campaign*, 1999

A tremendous myth has arisen around the importance of the third date in the modern era. Supposedly, the third date has been "anointed" with the mantle as the milepost at which time sexual intercourse will occur between a newly-dating couple. I've long heard of the myth; dates have even mentioned it to me, but I have never followed it. Each relationship develops on its own timetable. As I've said before, I've even had a couple of relationships that I hoped and expected would become long-term meaningful ones that were short-circuited because the sexual component emerged earlier than the woman wanted (even though she may have been as much as a progenitor as I in achieving the act). On the other hand, I have had serious, long-term (more than six months) relationships where no sexual intercourse took place. I have even spent the night with someone where this boundary was not crossed. So, there is no hard and fast rule; the chemistry between you two must be the guide, and you must both be willing to act as adults. You know the adage: the wonderful thing about being an adult is that you have the maturity to be able to say "no."

The question that I have to pose to you gents is this: if you have sex with this woman (and there is *no* question that since you're attracted to her and you clearly know by now that you share a lot of mutual interests that you *want* to), will that act completely take over all aspects of the relationship at this crucial time in the development of that association between the two of you? If the answer is yes, then (reluctantly) you should wait. Remember, you *are* an adult. But if the answer is no, then why not go ahead if it seems right. How do you know? Why, by all means, as with any development in this relationship, which as in any healthy relationship, major new activities are entered into after an overt and honest discussion between the two of you. And during this important chat, birth control should be discussed. Don't assume anything.

Remember, in your late teens/early twenties how often after the first time you were intimate with a new partner that, other than the sex, you really had nothing much to say or do with the gal? Well, you do not want that to happen here, right? You want to ensure that there is a firm foundation of friendship and mutual respect and attraction in place so that the sex really is literally the "icing on the cake," not the whole cake itself. So, why am I saying this in a tome intended generally for professionals in their thirties or forties? Because many men only see the "score" and not the awesome place that sex can play in a relationship – and a profound friendship – that has been firmly established already. Granted, some relationships are able to be built on and improved in both sexual and non-sexual aspects simultaneously. But most are not.

As an aside, let me stop here to respond to the question that some readers might have been asking themselves as they've read this book to this point: why do you keep talking about wine and never mention booze (hard stuff)? Easy, if the guy's over 40, wine will only enhance a man's sexual performance. Hard alcohol will only inhibit it. I've easily been able to split a bottle of wine and have never had my performance adversely affected. On the other hand, if I've even had one hard drink before dinner (with or without wine afterward), a negative effect often has resulted. Additionally, the high proof of the booze often wipes out one's palette, so that you cannot truly taste the wine – and that's a sin! So save the bourbon/scotch binges on nights out with the guys or when you're home alone unwinding after a hard day. The next time you're in a large mixed group, watch what everyone's drinking. I'll bet you anything that the married guys are slugging down the hard stuff, while the single guys are nursing a beer or a glass of wine. There's a reason for that, fella; the single guys want to be able to perform well later.

Besides, ask yourself the question: why is history and even the Bible replete with references to wine, not spirits? Because wine relaxes, bathes the two people having a conversation with a warm glow, and creates an atmosphere of intimacy. Wine give you a headache? Easy, stop drinking bad wine. Of good wines, only champagne will give you a headache. But you learned how to drink "plonk" in college, and you haven't grown out of it? Grow up. Spend $12-15 a bottle at least. You'll never get a headache again. Check out Appendix Two for recommendations on great moderately-priced wines

So, it's the third date. You both really like each other and can spend hours just talking. Should you go "all the way?" Again, talk about it. Be brutally honest but not so that you end up giving ultimatums or making her feel trapped. If, for any reason, she'd still rather wait, kiss her passionately and say, "Whatever makes you comfortable, honey. I'm ready when you are. I respect your decision." This is not a sex manual so I will refrain from offering physical solutions on how to get her to change her mind. But if she's really into you, there has to be something that is making her reticent, so just wait; it's only a matter of time.

If you mutually decide that it *is* time, then by all means take her out to dinner, watch your alcohol intake, and take her home. A mutual shower or bubble bath makes a great first step in the evening's festivities. Make sure you have plenty of candles, both by the tub and near the bed. Have your trusty, rusty boom box belting out Sade (playing "Smooth Operator"?) and slowly and sensually remove her clothes. She may attempt to takes yours off simultaneously, but tell her to wait. You want her to focus completely on the sensations that her own body will be feeling. Despite what Hollywood might impart, the first time with anybody is rarely an occasion where perfection in every respect is achieved. Don't worry about it; just make her feel special. The key is to focus on her pleasure, not yours. You're a guy; you're going to get your release, but a woman's body is far more complicated. It takes a knowledge of her anatomy, her physical likes and dislikes (and you don't know those yet), and how into you she is. Many women assume that the man really knows what he's doing, and you indeed may be quite experienced, but again, this is the first time with this lady. Ask her beforehand what she likes and dislikes. Before you try something new, ask her if she'd like such and such. Again, never assume anything. Talk to her and you'll get on the right plane with each other much more quickly.

One method to get things heated up expeditiously is to ensure that you're a good kisser. A good kisser rarely has trouble making his lady reach the ultimate of her passion. I had lots of practice kissing in college, as I apparently was a "virgin" magnet and had serious relationships with three outstanding ladies who each insisted on remaining virginal until marriage. That's not why we broke up, but I got lots of practice kissing. It was fun. Even in flight school I developed a relationship with a beautiful red head who really enjoyed necking but would permit nothing more. So, if you can add to this a skillful petting (not pawing, there *is* a difference) technique, and ease her body into a state where it craves more, you're headed in the right direction. Again, since this isn't a "how to" sex book I will refrain from more detailed discussion. Let it suffice to suggest that you read up on Tantric sex (two sources are included in the reading list in the appendix). This technique (actually a series of beliefs) focuses on spreading sexual energy from the erogenous zones to the entire body. It teaches you to enjoy sexual excitement without the normal sexual tension that normally is involved in an ever-increasing internal pressure that hopefully results in orgasm. Tantra teaches you to move this sexual energy – and even store it in the body – and to relax into a series of peaks of excitement. It even includes no-touch sexual orgasms, which frankly, is something I haven't tried.

It's likely that after the first intimate act that you won't spend the night together. If you don't expect to, it's no problem. If you do, great, and if the schedule permits, I strongly suggest a morning session of lovemaking, although if it's a weekday it'll be little more than a quickie. But it'll send both of you off to work with a post-coital glow.

Be sure and send her flowers the day after your first intimacy (or later the same day if you just left her bed that morning). While it's a nice touch; it's important. Make her more than glad that she slept with you. Ensure that she's thinking that you're not just another guy. Get her to think that you're special. She's special. So are you.

One of the key elements in helping to build an intimate relationship with a woman is the ability to engage in intimate conversation. Some guys never learn this; after all, it's counter-intuitive to the way guys think and talk. From the earliest ages, women grow up engaging in detailed and intricate conversations with their best friends about everything, especially about boys. Ever see the "Defending the Caveman" show? I've seen it four times! The reason that one-man play is so successful is that the creator has the stereotypes down pat. The point here is that the part of his soliloquy about guys talking together is right on. Two best friends don't see each other for a number of years, but when they finally get together it's like they never left each other. When they do encounter each other, it's a hit on the shoulder, and a "So, what's ya' been doin', dumb shit?" Real detailed dialogue, right?

Well, what a woman wants and expects is for you to "lower your guard" and really talk to her. This is especially true right after sex. Contrary to the Hollywood stereotype, the last thing you want to do after the physical act is to roll over and go to sleep. That will earn you more negative points than I can count. A woman wants you to cuddle her, to stroke her, and to talk softly to her. It doesn't have to be a rehash of what took place (other than to reassure her that it was wonderful). Rather, just tell her how special she is, how good she makes you feel, and how happy you are that you are together. You must be careful not to transcend how you really feel at the moment, but talk about the future and the things you'd like to do with her (not necessarily sexual) and the places you'd like to take her. This is called building intimacy and no amount of compatibility can exceed the positive aspects of creating and increasing the intimacy developed over the minutes of pillow talk in which you've engaged. Although I'm not a real country music fan, one lady bought me a

John Michael Montgomery cassette tape because it contained a song entitled "You Talk to Me" which extolled the virtues of this practice. I heartily, heartily recommend it, the practice that is, not necessarily the song.

Another way to increase intimacy, with or without intercourse, is to give each other massages. I recommend you volunteer to give her one first and don't be surprised or disappointed if, the first time, she never gets around to giving you one. But even if you've not yet decided to take your relationship to the next level and have sex, massages are a good way to express your feelings physically and to get to know each others' bodies better, short of the act of intercourse itself. You don't even need the right equipment; all you need is a towel (laid on the floor or the bed) and baby oil. Once you're really into each other, I would invest in some fragrant massage oil, but there's no need to buy a massage table or some such. As will be discussed in the next chapter, massages are also a great way to keep your relationship refreshed as there are so many different massage styles and methods. It's fun to experiment.

Chapter Seven
Making Your Lady Feel Special

"Honesty is the only way with anyone, when you'll be so close as to be living inside each other's skins."

Lois McMaster Bujold, *A Civil Campaign*, 1999

So, other than keeping her sexually satisfied – once you've decided that it was appropriate to move the relationship up to that plane – how do you continue to make your lady feel special? And trust me, buddy, if you are not satisfying her physically, red flags will be raised in her mind that you're not *it*. This chapter will make you glad you spent the money to buy this book.

First, let's talk about some obvious things that guys do when they're teenagers but somehow feel it's uncool to do when they're older. Women love to hear two things: that you love them and that they look great. When's the last time you said something like that to the last person with whom you had a meaningful relationship? Smart guys say something along those lines every day. You're *never* too busy to tell the person who's most important to your life about how you feel about them and to compliment them. Even CEOs and Presidents do that, the smart ones anyway. The other thing is to express little physical signs of affection, like holding hands. Embarrassed to show public displays of affection? OK, but what's wrong with holding her hand while you're driving or just sitting there watching television? It means that you're comforted by her presence and touching her makes her feel closer to you. Walking down the street with your hand on her shoulder or even around her waist is another such sign. Lightly rubbing her arm or the top of her thigh while you're sitting together is another similar such sign, and you're not rubbing her leg to get her turned on; you're just expressing affection. Women love it and deserve to be shown such treatment.

You've heard of frequent flyer miles, right? Did you know that there was such a thing as "frequent flower miles?" Yep, there is. I used to belong to two such programs. When should you send flowers? I didn't know you needed a reason. OK, OK, OK, so you do. Well, here are a few: after the first date or before the second, after the first dinner, after the first dinner she cooked for you, after the first bout of sex, after the first away weekend (discussed below), after the first trip one of you took without the other, before any major or stress-causing event in her life (hopefully one not caused by you), after the first fight. Need I go on? If she takes a business trip, call her secretary/assistant (you do know her by now, don't you? This person can make or break your relationship – hell, send her flowers on a *rare* occasion – and you should know the names of her kids and other important aspects of her life. One friend of mine, a lobbyist for a big oil company, developed this trait (not a trick, he was really that great of a guy) and he would know policy/political things before literally anyone else in town, because he treated the secretaries as the most important people in town) and find out the name of the hotel where your lady is staying. A quick phone call, and, viola!, flowers waiting in her room. Is she going on a cruise with her college roommates or her family. Presto! Order up one of those old-movie Bon Voyage bouquets for her cabin. It's not to make all her friends jealous of her (and their significant others will be hateful of you), but this is the lady of your life, dude. She's worth it. And if you don't think, so, then trust me, she's not the lady you're meant to be with forever. Going on a trip yourself? Stop at that little flight insurance kiosk in the airport and buy a $10,000 accident insurance policy.

Name her as the beneficiary and have the paperwork sent to her (pre-paid, you jerk!).

Many people are clueless what to buy their girlfriend for Valentine's Day. Problem solved. Buy her a high class evening handbag from a major department store (the kind that is barely large enough to hold more than a compact and a tube of lipstick). Fill it with Hershey's candy kisses. Nothing more need be said. Of course, this is also a day to get another couple of numbers punched in your frequent flowers card. But any man who buys his lady mass-market candy from a drug store for Valentine's Day needs holes drilled in his head. As a matter of fact, *never* buy that kind of candy unless you're trying to send the message that you really don't care. Because that *is* the message that they receive – plus, that you're a dolt. Now, if she's diabetic or something, I think that a drug store is probably the only kind of store in which you can buy sugar-free chocolates (and believe it or not, some of those are fairly good if you must eat them). But other than such exceptions, go to a department store and buy Belgian or Swiss chocolate – or Godiva (which has a great website), of course. It's really worth it, and it does show you care.

Cards. Did I mention I owned stock in Hallmark? No, but sometimes I wish I did! Shortly after the first or second date, visit your local card store. Now, usually the chain drug stores don't have the cards you need; they're after the masses. This lady you're wooing ain't part of the masses, pal. She's special. So find a card store that's edgy; that's in; that sells cards for those "who get it." Visit it once or twice a month and stock up. Don't start out with the mushy cards, you idiot; you're not in middle school any more. Send the ones (never more than 1 or 2 per week, you're wooing her, not stalking her) that say you're thinking of her; you think she's special (or might become special), that kind of message. If either of you is about to take a trip, send one that will arrive at her home and be waiting her return that says you missed her. You might even mail one ahead of time to her out-of-town hotel (help from that friendly assistant again; buddy, you want her to be your biggest fan!), so it's awaiting her at check-in. Only after you're convinced you're really in love start with the mushy ones, and if the physical part of your relationship has kicked in you can add in the kind (but don't *only* send those kind) that are highly suggestive or downright blunt, but ones your lover will appreciate. But be discrete; this isn't a fraternity gross-out. It's meant to show your sense of humor and thoughtfulness.

In addition to store bought cards, occasionally make one. The computer is a marvelous tool and you don't have to be a commercial artist to make artistic and thoughtful ones. Are you a computer illiterate? Fine, find a friend with a Mac (which all computer design people use) and have them make one for you. Besides that, once in awhile leave a hand-written note in her pocket, purse, or briefcase. Just imagine the look on her face at the next day's business meeting when a yellow sticky falls out of her briefcase and she picks it up to read "I love you" or "I'm thinking of you" in your hand writing. Her lingerie drawer is a good place to leave either such notes or store bought cards. Just make sure your relationship has progressed to a point where she won't be upset that you opened that drawer! If not, leave it in her bedside stand or even in her kitchen silverware drawer (if she lives alone).

The first time either of you meets the other's parents is always a noteworthy event; one that should be planned for in advance for you to come across at your best. Now, most of us who've had extensive dating experience going back to high school have gotten the "meet the parents" thing down pretty well, but if you've had bad luck in this department, then by all means plan it out ahead of time. Ask your lady ahead of time what she's told them about you so you know what areas to bring up and which they already know. If her parents live in the area, it's not as big a thing. Sometime in the first one or two months of the relationship, she's bound to invite you over to a family dinner. Dress sharply, but don't overdress. Find out ahead of time what the entrée will be and take an appropriate bottle of wine. Take her mother a flower or a small flowering plant. If her father smokes cigars, by all means take him a couple; he may even offer to give you one back to smoke with him on the back porch. The main thing is to be yourself, again being careful not to be a motor-mouth talking about yourself incessantly. If it's your folks she's meeting, tell them a little about your lady ahead of time, but don't give them a full-fledged dossier so they can ask her some polite questions themselves to get to know her at their own speed. Put your lady at ease by describing your parents beforehand and sharing some of their likes and dislikes (about things in general, not about the women you've introduced them to in the past).

If her parents live out of town, see the chapter below about spending the first Christmas with them for suggestions on how you should comport yourself. Again, the key is to be relaxed and yourself.

One of the true tests of a new relationship is the road trip. Many a nascent relationship has blown up because in the normal dating world, you've never spent more than a few hours together at a time, but a weekend away involves dozens of hours together that may enlighten one or both of you to the fact that you can only stand each other for a few hours at a time! Now, if you've been making sojourns down to the boat, this hurdle should have already been successfully cleared, but if not, get prepared. The two of you will know when it's wise to attempt it. Now you may be constrained, schedule-wise, on when and if you can get away. One or both of you may have kids that you have custody of that may preclude you from going away. But sooner or later the opportunity will present itself and, hopefully, the two of you will have discussed it and will be ready to act on it when that happens. If your lady has family in the area, they will only be more than happy to watch her kids for a weekend, especially as they have seen how happy you make her. If they don't see that, then you aren't doing your job, bub.

A weekend trip (and I recommend the first one only entail one or two nights, as even pleasurable times need to be gradually eased into) can be simply a drive to an away city, a train ride (not nearly as romantic as they must have been a hundred years ago with parlor cars, etc.), a plane trip (again, not as much fun as pre-9/11), a visit to old friends of one of you, an away college reunion, a camping trip, or even a weekend away on your yacht (not recommended as a first weekend away). What I strongly recommend for a first time away together is a Saturday morning drive an hour or three away to either the mountains or the coast, and a sleepover at a bed and breakfast. In the fall or early spring, the ocean is fun. Long walks along the beach and/or boardwalk, uncrowded due to its being off-season, evenings before a fire (hopefully in your bedroom), a wonderful meal of seafood in town, and all the other normal accoutrements of a romantic weekend. The fall is obviously great for mountain B&Bs, and I prefer the mountains for both the dead of winter and summer for obvious but different reasons.

As the guy, you should check her schedule getting multiple holes on her calendar. Schedule the one that seems best for the time of year (and your budget, if that's an issue, but count on spending at least $200-300/night for a decent B&B), and gas up the car. Now, the extras that make the difference between you and the rest of the poor schmucks out there who are just trailing in your wake: If you are going up on Friday, and the area has the amenities (and your lady is into either), book a tee time at the nearby golf course or a court time at the local tennis court. If need be, borrow the extra set of clubs or racket if your lady doesn't already own hers. If you're not going to a B&B, select a hotel that has a pool (and hopefully a hot tub), then remind her to take a suit.

But you should *never* go on a weekend away anywhere (except to her parents' house) without at least one candle (I like the 3 to 4 inch diameter ones that will burn all night, and especially those with a scent like raspberry, and they don't require a candle holder). You also should never venture on such an excursion without a small, high quality CD/cassette player and at least one CD/tape by Sade and Andrea Bocelli. The old guys swore by Ravel's *Bolero*. I swear by Sade (pronounced *shar day*), the Nigerian torch singer, and Bocelli, the blind Italian tenor with the golden voice. I've been told more than once by female music store clerks that ladies like Sarah McLachlan for romantic interludes, so what the hey; throw in a couple of hers. The whole point is to set the mood and to create an unforgettable weekend.

Rounding out the magic triad of things to take is a miniature cooler with two splits of champagne (I recommend Perrier Jouet Grand Brut, less than $20/split). I recommend splits because they're smaller than a regular champagne bottle and easier to transport and, let's face it, you're not trying to get either of you snockered; it's to help set the mood. Don't forget the glasses. Don't take expensive lead crystal flutes, but plastic and paper cups don't cut it with champagne. In a pinch the supplied bathroom glasses will do, if they're made of glass, but you can't depend on that and the proprietor will think you're really weird if you call ahead to inquire if your bathroom's drinking glasses will be made of glass!

Hopefully, you can get a bedroom with a fireplace. Except for the summer, they can be used all year round and they really set a romantic mood. If you drive down on a Saturday morning, check in and immediately go to the room lugging your stuff. Lock the door and make passionate love to her right on the floor. This connotes that not only are you glad she's with you, but "honey, this is going to be a weekend you're never going to forget." Don't worry if it's not romantic, violin-playing lovemaking; that will come later. This is a welcome-to-our-weekend baby, kind of sex – the purely lustful kind that you had in your twenties but rarely do any more because you know the more tender kind is better.

Get cleaned up, and maybe she'll want to take a short nap atop the covers, but just spoon. Get up, but before you go downstairs, give her a gift that you've bought for her for that weekend. It could be a little book of poetry; it could be a special clip for her hair; it could be a broach for her shawl if it's cool out; it could be a dinner outfit for that night – but do it! Then go downstairs and chat up the proprietor and his wife (they're usually interesting people, if for no other reason than they're exposed to so many interesting people, but most are well-traveled), tour the grounds, and maybe drive into the local community to visit the sites (ask your hosts, as they know which ones are open, which ones are having sales, where the community events are, where the historical sites are, and where the best place to have dinner is (ask them if they'd kindly call for you to make a reservation at their best table)). Shoot for dinner around 8 p.m., then go out with your lady and enjoy the things your host has suggested in which you both have an interest.

Come back to your room and as you're getting dressed, give her the second gift that you've gotten for her to commemorate that weekend. I prefer a matching Victoria's Secret lingerie set – nothing slutty like from Frederick's of Hollywood, but something sexy, yet classy. She'll love it and, hopefully, she'll put it on under her dinner outfit, but hey, she may have already brought something special for that purpose. If you don't know her size, then shame on you; you shouldn't be on this weekend; it's too early and you're rushing it, you moron. Anyhow, enjoy dinner. Remember, the wine is the most important thing about the dinner. While I enjoy food as much as the next person, and if you saw me any doubt to that effect would be erased, but looking back, I remember the lady I was with and the wine; rarely the food.

After dinner, come back to the room, undress down to your skivvies (her in her new "gift"), and sit together on the floor in front of the fireplace with the two splits of champagne. Hopefully, the conversation at dinner has led you both to a warm and fuzzy point, where you're now just grooving on each other and the ambience of the venue. If the floor is uncomfortable, use either one of the B&B's blankets or even your winter coat if it's that time of year. This time is for silent whispers, cuddles, passionate kisses, and petting. Once things take hold, adjourn to the bed, pausing to light the candles and to turn on Sade. Her melodic tones will smooth the transition into a night of passion neither of you will forget.

In the morning, try to awaken first, throw on your robe, and scoot downstairs to bring her up a cup of coffee in bed. You have been paying attention and know how she likes it don't you? You don't? What are you, a self-centered jerk? Boy, your mother sure spoiled you, pal, get over yourself! If possible, bring back an entire tray with two plates of breakfast on it (some B&Bs permit it; others don't). Hopefully there are some strawberries or orange sections so you can feed those to her hand-to-mouth. Some people prefer making love in the morning. Whether this is true for either of you, what better time and place to practice? Check out is usually around noon, so go for it. See if you can use tantric methods to make one single union last until 11:45 a.m.!! Right before you leave the room, give her the third and last gift you've brought for her: a desk sized framed photo of you both. It will most likely be an informal shot of you both if it's to be a surprise, as any formal pose clearly would not be. When she puts that on her office desk or her bedside stand it will always remind her of this weekend.

While I wouldn't recommend this "full court" treatment every time you both visit a B&B (after all you wanted that first weekend away to be really special, right?), but you can always have a little special gift in your bag to present to her on any overnight trip away from home. Again, this separates you from the rest of the slugs she's dated in the past.

Another type of weekend might entail a day trip to a historical site. Civil war battle sites are my favorite. They're educational and provide an opportunity to spend a long time together without talking.

Remember that if this is to be a long-term, meaningful relationship, companionship is an extremely important trait that is essential for the relationship to work. No historical sites near you? Then try a visit to a number of wineries and do a bit of judicious tasting. Almost every state now has a winery and California, Oregon, Washington, New York, Maryland, and Virginia are replete with them. Do your homework beforehand online and map out a route to take in as many wineries as you can within the available time. Be careful not to get soused; that's not the purpose of the trip. You'll want to buy a bottle or two of the best wines you taste. You can even have a case or two shipped directly to your house unless you live in one of those Medieval states that don't allow it.

Still another type of weekend can be, assuming that neither of your abodes has a Jacuzzi, at a hotel a couple of times a year that has one in the room. The hotel can even be local. Insist that the Jacuzzi be big enough to hold two people. It's a fantastic experience on a cold, Friday night to have a light dinner and then adjourn to the Jacuzzi with two snifters of brandy (or Armagnac, which tastes much like brandy yet doesn't contain the high alcoholic content that causes headaches in some people). Of course, you will have brought a couple of your candles and the music player. You just might find after the bubble bath that you're way too relaxed to do anything but sleep. If you find that distasteful you can always dry each other off to get the blood (and other body parts) flowing.

Either on the Jacuzzi weekend or just a night back at home, massages are a special treat rather than immediately jumping into bed together. Always give her one first, as, you animal, you *know* that once she gets a certain part of your anatomy aroused that all bets are off as far as just massaging each other. The skin is the largest organ of the human body and some people feel that it's the largest erogenous zone. Caressing it causes certain hormones to be released into the body that simultaneously brings relaxation and excitement (it depends on the type of touch, not necessarily where that touch was administered). Slow and deliberate massages bring sort of a meditation to the body; what better way to help unwind each other after your stressful weeks than a mutual massage? More on this in Chapter Eight.

Finally, I used to make a special night out of evenings when there was a full moon. Either we'd take a stroll in the moonlight (I found *the* bench on the National Mall from which to view the full moon passing directly over top of the Washington Monument about 8:45 p.m. in August), have a restaurant meal at a sidewalk café, or take a moonlight sail. Even if the full moon were on a weeknight, I would pick up my lady after work, having first gone to a deli for a picnic dinner and picnic wine, and drive to the sailboat. We'd cast off and sail for an hour until the moon was nice and high. Then I'd throw out the anchor, drop the sails, and break out the picnic dinner. Since the boat is not underway, you can eat food that is not necessarily "finger food," which is what you are usually limited to when you have lunch underway while sailing. We'd usually be home by midnight, but there were fewer evenings as romantic as that.

Chapter Eight
Keeping the Relationship Fresh

"...you shall be together even in the silent memory of God. But let there be spaces in your togetherness. And let the winds of the heavens dance between you."

Kahil Gibran, *The Prophet*

I t's clear that you two now have something great. You think you might even be in love. You might even be discussing meeting each other's folks if they reside out of town. How do you keep it fresh? The enemy of any relationship is complacency. Complacency is brought on by routine, familiarity, and boredom. These are some key activities that can help you avoid routine and ennui and thus keep your relationship fresh while you continue to build and grow it.

Again, I like to eat as much as the next guy, but you can spend every penny of your disposable income buying the two of you dinner unless you can think of innovative ways to minimize the expense. The best way, as I've said before, is to learn how to cook, but when you do go out, try this to save a little money: most movie houses have a reduced twilight rate. Unless you're meeting a crowd of people at the show, go to the earlier showing and have dinner afterwards at some informal place. That way you're not rushing your meal so as not to be late for the beginning of the movie. Plus, you're often so full from the movie popcorn that you both eat a far smaller restaurant meal.

Regarding a home-cooked meal, the traditional way among most of us chauvinistic American males is to expect the lady to cook for us, but I never assumed that that would happen. If it did occur, appreciate the heck out of it (and always take a very good quality wine to accompany the meal and always ask what else you can bring) and show your appreciation. But there are sometimes circumstances that make it rare or impossible for your lady to cook for you at her place. If she asks you if it's OK to cook you a meal at your house, readily agree. Don't be getting all territorial about your kitchen and its implements. Say, "Sure!"

But usually if she asked what we should do at our next get together, I'd say, "Bring a DVD and join me for dinner." If she offers to bring wine, also readily agree. If you imply that your cellar contains quality wines that are preferable to anything she'd bring, she may never again offer – or worse – be intimidated sufficiently that she'll never buy you wine as a gift. One of the most fun gifts to receive is a nice (not necessarily, expensive) bottle of wine – because the possibilities are endless. The default dinner in my kitchen was boneless chicken breasts. There's even a book on "101 Ways to Cook Chicken." But the ol' standby was simply cooking two succulent chicken breasts in butter and garlic and onions and white wine. Easy and delicious. Serve it with plain buttered noodles or one of the prepared rice dinners that you just pop in the microwave for a couple of minutes. Of course the wine would be a good mid-priced Chardonnay. For a dinner salad, as a variation from lettuce, serve washed spinach leaves, canned Mandarin orange sections, sliced almonds, and peppercorn dressing. Or instead of the spinach leaves, cut up an avocado in season, and serve with the oranges, almonds, and the peppercorn dressing (or as a variation, serve sweet and sour dressing). The combination of tastes is exquisite. Another type salad that most people have never had is a Madrid salad: cut up extremely ripe tomatoes and onions, drained tuna, and olive oil. For dessert, after dinner heat a can of cherries and their juice with a half cup each of sugar and corn starch and stir constantly until the mixture becomes thickened (don't burn it). Serve it warm over vanilla ice cream. Delicious.

In the summer, invite another couple and throw on the grill a whole salmon that the store has cleaned (gutted and de-scaled, but with the head intact). Stuff it with crabmeat and wrap it in tin foil and cook 20 minutes on each side. Serve it with white rice or Spanish rice. I have had friends who do not like fish rave over this meal. In addition to Chardonnay, a good Pinot Noir is a good match for salmon. With other fish, especially shell fish, I only serve Sauvignon Blanc or a California Fume Blanc or perhaps a Pinot Grigio, as they are crisper and steelier. The reason I suggest another couple is the salmon is sufficiently large for four people. In the summer, buy a dozen hard crabs from a good crab house or from a fresh seafood store. They must be kept alive (eating dead ones that you have cooked can make you very sick), but that's not hard. Storing them in a paper sack with wet newspaper at the top is usually sufficient. Boil them with Old Bay spice and either white vinegar or beer for seven minutes and boy, what a treat. Serve them with corn on the cob and beer. Serve them with your entire table covered with layers of newspaper (outside on a picnic table is best). Have hammers, pliers and/or nut crackers and tiny forks to dig out the meat from the claws and legs. Once a year get two large (1 ½ to 3 pound) lobsters from a fresh seafood market (if you're anywhere on the East Coast in the Mid-Atlantic or Northeast there *has* to be at least one market that trucks lobsters in weekly from Maine). Steam them for seven minutes and serve with butter you've melted in a double boiler. Serve with corn on the cob and/or boiled potatoes and a crisp white wine – Pouilly fume or Sauvignon Blanc. The best fresh fish widely available these days is tilapia. It is a non-smelly whitefish that is delicate and delicious. Stuff it with crab meat or wild rice, broil it, and you have a stunning meal.

If you're both so worn out from your busy work weeks that there's literally no way either of you can cook (and you're not in the mood to go out), stop by Safeway on your way home. They have the most amazing 24" diameter pizza that's always on sale on Friday. Can't beat it for $6.99, and a similar quality one would cost at least $15 if delivered. After the pizza, enjoy either a DVD, an evening playing cards, or an hour in the Jacuzzi while enjoying snifters of brandy or vintage port.

As a diversion, occasionally cook your lady breakfast. No, it doesn't always have to be breakfast in bed, though that earns you more points. Start with a champagne glass with a canned peach half and champagne. An alternative would be to also add orange juice. Then serve ham and cheese omelets cooked in a bit of white wine. Garnish them with baby croissants or blueberry muffins. Once in awhile, instead of omelets, make quiche. It's really not that hard to do, and in a pinch store-bought ones are usually of sufficient quality that don't disappoint. A third option is either scrambled eggs with canned beanless chili served as gravy over the eggs or fried eggs with left-over enchiladas (my family's favorite). Fresh ground coffee or instant cappuccino (unless you happen to own an expresso/cappucciono machine) completes your tray. If it's Sunday, by all means spend the day in bed eating, reading the newspaper, and loving.

One interesting diversion that can help keep your relationship fresh is to go out dancing. While what immediately comes to mind is going to a club, those can get old, especially as you watch "players" continue to work the meat market. There *are* other alternatives. One is a country and western bar where the two of you can learn to do the "two-step." It's really fun. Another is to learn which of the major hotels in your area have late night swing dancing. Some of these hotels bring in a DJ after 10 p.m. for people to swing dance, although it may be on a weeknight. At first you're intimidated by the seemingly-professional dance moves being exhibited but after you watch the dancers for awhile, a reasonably proficient dancer should be able to pick up some moves. Besides, it's just for fun; no one is judging you. If you're still intimidated, take a swing dancing class together; still another way of keeping your relationship refreshed. My experience at these hotels is a good one. The room is kept fairly dark, and the room is never crowded (though the dance floor might be). This affords an intimacy rare at such a venue than is present at most other times. There is no continuous pressure for you to imbibe too much and the whole evening (usually starting after the dinner hour) is a very enjoyable one, enabling the two of you to get even more into each other.

I've touched on these before, but interesting day trips keep your times together from becoming stale. There are published one-day trip books available for most major metropolitan areas. Antique shops, nature parks/trails, state parks, lakes, mountains, scenic vistas, and/or historic sites all offer interesting diversions. My favorite are Civil War sites, usually those centered around battles. Some enable you to tour from the comfort of your car. Others have dioramas or other multi-media productions. Some entail a great deal of walking. Either check them out on the internet or call the information center beforehand if there are limitations guiding your choice of activity.

While theme parks offer an all-day experience, these could require a great deal of standing in line, so ensure you're up to the rigors and that the weather will cooperate. If the park has any sort of water ride, be sure to advise her to bring another outfit to don should she become soaked.

Either play golf or tennis once in awhile or take lessons so you become more adept at both. Remember, golf is an activity that you can play as long as you can walk. It also could involve a great deal of time riding together on an electric cart, so if your hectic week has limited your time to chat, over 18 holes you're all caught up! Some courses also permit the viewing of some outstanding scenery; such experiences are always more pleasurable when you're able to share them with someone special. Depending on the course, you either get lunch delivered to you by the "snack cart," or you can dash into the club at the turn to grab two sandwiches, chips, and two drinks. A beer afterwards to re-hydrate is a perfect ending. An alternative is miniature golf. You can keep it fun if you don't get too competitive and insist on winning. Don't throw the match, but don't get so serious that it isn't fun for her. One way to mitigate that is to take along local nieces and nephews, if neither of you have your own offspring. It will also serve to show her that you're into kids.

One of the advantages of tennis is that it doesn't involve as much time (either in the distances involved in reaching the site or in the time it takes to play). Granted tennis is not that much fun if there is a wide disparity between your abilities, but c'mon what is this, Wimbledon? Play two or three vigorous sets, then adjourn to lunch – or just a couple of beers.

Another interesting evening can involve attending a charity auction. Wine auctions for charity are especially fun, but they involve imbibing large amounts of free wine so you may end up spending more than you intended. If you are worried about this happening take up to $200 cash but leave your credit cards and check book at home. What should you bid on? My favorite are the silent auctions featuring donated services from the "service" industry. A "free" limo ride, a "free" night at a local luxury hotel, a "free" meal at a swanky restaurant, or a "free" week or weekend at a resort/timeshare someplace fun. If you can't hold one yourself, you might want to bid on a free wine tasting where a wine expert comes to your home and conducts a wine tasting for you and your friends. I've offered those myself at fundraising events at my church and children's school where I conduct the wine tasting for 8 people at the couple's house and they invite their own friends. They make for very fun evenings.

One type of dinner that will keep your relationship refreshed is a "mystery dinner." Normally, this entails going to a restaurant that features this attraction. Often these are in long-established restaurants in large, old houses that are past their prime with respect to being an "in" place to eat. To stay in business, they have added the "mystery dinner" to keep patrons coming in. You have a dinner while a set of actors enacts the mystery and by the time dessert is served the audience is somehow engaged in either the action or in guessing who the culprit is. Now, these can be a simple dinner theater type affair or even on a train. In any event, they're fun. Another alternative is to host your own "mystery dinner." You can buy at party stores or online the game box with all the instructions. You invite 8-12 people and assign them roles. Some come with guidance on costumes people should wear, but that's just an option. It's quite fun, but sometimes you have participants who don't quite get into the thing and it brings it down, so choose your invitees carefully.

Obviously, throwing any type of party can help keep your relationship refreshed. You must first decide between yourselves whose home will be the party site. Then decide how large, whom to invite, what to serve, and whether there shall be a theme (toga, costume, Roaring 20s, 50s, etc.). All this can be stressful if the two of you are still working out your roles within the relationship. Ideally, you have developed into a couple where neither needs to be dominant and you are readily able to make decisions together. It's not a good idea to co-host a party unless it is widely known that the two of you are a "couple." If not, and for one reason or another, one of you doesn't want the fact known to certain people it can get really awkward, so tread carefully.

There are all kinds of theme parties that are fun: costume parties, scavenger hunts, '50s or '60s parties, etc. The benefit of having your lady involved with the planning is that women are usually far more imaginative than we mere guys, and they sure have a flair for decorating. You be in charge of picking the liquid libation, determining what drinks to serve, how much, and where to purchase it. Let her have the lead in deciding what food to serve, but by all means chip in on shopping, paying for, and fixing it. This type of activity is instrumental in demonstrating to each of you how well you work together. The best relationships are ones where the two partners complement, not necessarily overlap each other's skills. If you can't work together, that says something too, but not necessarily that you won't work out as a couple. We've all known long-time married couples who would never dream of working together professionally.

A fun day that will build (and test) your ability to work together as a team is the road rally. Research the web to find the numerous car and road rally clubs sponsoring such events in your area. You do not need a fast car, but it's more fun in good weather to be in a sports car and/or in a convertible. The participants are started in a stagger; you receive a packet containing clues, riddles, or puzzles that you must figure out and follow to know which turns to make, distances to drive, and roads to follow. There are numerous checkpoints at which you must check in and sometimes pick up additional clue-containing packets. Such rallies usually last several hours, culminating at a bar or restaurant where the participants compare war stories of their days' adventures. It's usually loads of fun. A newer version is "geocaching" in which you online are given certain GPS coordinates (obviously you need a GPS receiver to play, but the cost of those is finally reasonable) and the first person to reach the spot finds a minor gift or prize. Sometimes the spot also contains GPS coordinates to the next spot and so on. They're quite fun.

Sporting events themselves are also a wonderful way to spend the day. If you both went to the same school, you are already provided with a mutual interest for which you both can root. If you went to rival schools, an interesting dynamic will develop, but remember, don't take it so seriously that you damage your relationship over a damned game. Introduce her to sports with which she may not be as familiar, such as lacrosse, which is both fast and exciting. If you don't know the rules, check a book on the game out of the library so you can be more conversant on what's going on with respect to tactics and referees' calls. I once was with a lady who would even intimidate most guys with her intricate knowledge of football rules and tactics. It was fun to watch. After an all-day sporting event, such as an away football game, call your local pizza delivery place and have a pizza waiting for you at home (or her place). Only a Neanderthal would expect his lady to cook for him after an exhausting day out. Dude, she's as tired as you are!

As much as I love football, there is nothing like attending a baseball game to help build greater intimacy between a couple. The game's more leisurely pace affords an opportunity to cuddle, hold hands, and whisper sweet things into her ear. You're not jumping to your feet every few minutes, and you can really settle in together. A minor league game is even more fun (and cheaper!), as things seem more relaxed, family oriented, and designed to entertain the fans without such an emphasis on the home team's winning.

Lastly, we come again to the subject of massage. Massage should be one of the key elements in keeping your relationship refreshed. Many couples try it once or twice, but since most people really don't know what they're doing they soon stop. Either read some books or watch some videos to get techniques and tricks to keep your massage activities honed and toned. The result will bring you long-lasting results.

Both parties should always take a bath or shower before you start. If you have coitus in the shower, some of the sexual tension that quickly rises during the massage will be dissipated, so that you can focus on truly giving your partner a thorough massage. Start with her hands and feet. Some experts say you should spend twenty minutes on these appendages alone prior to beginning massage on the main part of the torso.

Massage, like kissing, is even more intimate between two people than intercourse is. Make sure the room is warm, you have your scented candles alight, and Sade or a piano concerto playing in the background. Find the biggest, fluffiest towel you have and have her lie down face first on it. Begin by massaging both sides of her spine down to her lower back. Slowly and thoroughly caress her shoulders and upper back with special emphasis on her neck. Much daily stress is stored in the muscles of the neck and this requires continuous firm stroking, caressing, and squeezing to release it. Gently massage her calves and the back of her thighs, purposefully avoiding the buttocks and the inside of her legs. After twenty to thirty minutes, have her gently turn over. Begin to focus on the center of her chest, avoiding her breasts for now. With the palm of your hands, make circular motions around her chest, pushing the blood away from her heart. Move slowly down to her stomach and pubic bone, continually making circular motions with your palms. Then, without lifting your hands from her body, move your hands down to her ankles, and slowly massage the inside of her legs. Slowly move up the inside of her legs (the softest skin on a woman's body is on the inside of her legs at thigh-level) to her pubic area. The rest is up to you. Of course, the whole time you should be *gently* blowing in her ears (a very erogenous spot for many women) and whispering sweet nothings as you proceed.

Chapter Nine
Special Days that Can Make or Break a Relationship

"How can a woman be expected to be happy with a man who insists on treating her as if she were a perfectly normal human being?"

Oscar Wilde

"Find a guy who calls you beautiful instead of hot, who calls you back when you hang up on him, who will lie under the stars and listen to your heartbeat, or will stay awake just to watch you sleep... wait for the boy who kisses your forehead, who wants to show you off to the world when you are in sweats, who holds your hand in front of his friends, who thinks you're just as pretty without makeup on. One who is constantly reminding you of how much he cares and how lucky he is to have you.... The one who turns to his friends and says, 'that's her.'"

Sam Wilson

There are special days in everyone's lives that, when handled properly, deepen and enrich meaningful relationships, but when fumbled, can end a nascent bond between two people. Among these are birthdays, Christmas, and New Year's. We've already

63

discussed Valentine's Day, so while that day falls into this category, the discussion about it will not be repeated here. Some ladies put a great deal of importance on the day you first met or on the anniversary of your first date. If your lady does, so should you. If not, let it go.

Birthdays are special; even if someone insists that they aren't, trust me, they are. And if someone is supposedly the special lady in your life, then Charlie, you better treat that day as a special one. If her friends have to plan something because you're a doofus and don't pick up on the "specialness" of the day, then lots of red flags are going to go up in their minds that perhaps you really don't think that their gal is that special. A party is not necessarily required. However, if your wonderful woman has a close set of friends who always throw each other birthday parties, then by all means go along with it. Don't take it over (the "controlling" label will immediately be applied to you), but sit down with them over a cup of coffee/glass of wine and find out what they have in mind. By all means chime in with your two cents, and don't expect that you'll have to pick up the tab for the whole shebang. One fun type party is a '50s party at a neighborhood swimming pool (of course, someone in the group has to live in such a neighborhood for this to work). But it could be just a dozen close friends in her or your apartment. If it's to be a surprise, then you need these gals' input in spades: in terms of whom to invite, when and where to have it, what to serve, and the schedule that day to spring the surprise on her. Don't forget her able assistant/secretary who again can be invaluable to you in setting this up.

But of even greater importance is how you treat her and what you give her that will stick out most in her mind. I once knew someone who planned and executed a surprise black tie breakfast on a weekday morning for his special lady. She walked down the stairs to go to work, and there in the dining room were the four closest couples in their lives resplendent in tuxes and gowns. The formal china was laid out and, boy, did he hit a homerun. I assume he had it catered, as the noise attendant to cooking breakfast for that many people surely would have tipped her off. I've also heard of another such catered, formal birthday breakfast being held on the pavement between the Lincoln Memorial and the reflecting pool on the National Mall, but the political pull and security arrangements now required as a result of 9/11 may preclude another one of those.

Ideally her birthday doesn't occur earlier than two or three months into the relationship. Before that and it would be awkward and maybe even inappropriate to purchase a gift that is too personal or too expensive. It would seem to her as if you were rushing things, even if down deep in your gut you knew that this lady is "the one." Before that I wouldn't buy anything more expensive than, say, a Hermes scarf. Maybe a ring containing her birth stone would be nice. Jewelry is always a smart buy and most women enjoy receiving it; again, just be careful at the beginning of a relationship that you don't buy something too expensive. It will make her feel uncomfortable, as if you're trying to buy her love, or that you expect her to do something to "earn" such an expensive gift. You want her to like the gift without her feeling pressured. On the other hand, too "ordinary" a gift will also send a negative signal. If you truly have a committed relationship, however, the choices of what to buy are infinitely broader.

Personally, once the relationship is established I would buy her an entire outfit for her birthday: dress, bag, and shoes. Some guys might find that a bit challenging but, trust me, at a reputable department store the sales ladies will fall all over themselves trying to help you. Pick out the dress first (you do know her size don't you?). Although every designer cuts his/her fashions to fit a bit differently, if you know her size you're usually in good shape (if not, it's always safer to *underestimate* the size than to overestimate it: "How could you possibly think I'm a size 18, you cretin?!!"). In *addition to* the gift you purchase, an additional gift that shows a lot of care is a handwritten IOU. Not an IOU for money, but for a chore or a service. IOU's can be for a massage, for a house cleaning, for a car wash, for a meal when it's her-"turn"-but-she's-too-tired, or anything of that nature.

I once had a billionaire (yes, actually) advise me to never, but never buy your wife or girlfriend a household appliance for her birthday. He just blurted it out one day as we were riding in his car on the way to a business meeting. Seems to me he must have made that mistake one time. As commonsensical as it seems, apparently even billionaire men can be clods when it comes to buying their ladies a gift!

In addition to the gift and flowers (again, the "frequent flower" card comes in handy), obviously, you'll want to either take her to dinner or to fix her a special one yourself. This is one of those occasions when it's totally proper to buy a more expensive bottle of wine at the restaurant. Restaurants typically raise the price of a bottle 300% for wines costing under $25 retail and 200% for more expensive wines. So, if you see a $60 bottle on the menu, you can probably buy it for $30 or so at a good wine store.

Remember the "silent" auctions mentioned in the last chapter? This would be an exemplary time to trot out some of the things you won there. Assuming you won the silent auction on the limousine service, have it pick you both up at her place. If you have time, have the car take you on a quick scenic tour around your city or through the countryside. Inside you have stocked a bottle of champagne on ice (most Americans drink their red wine too warm and their white wines too cold, but you can *never* drink champagne too cold). But plan the drive so that you're not late for your dinner reservation. The reservation can be at a restaurant where you also won a "free" meal, but that's not necessary. It's even more romantic if it's at a restaurant in the country, maybe at a country inn. If the latter, don't book a room as then you're without transportation the next morning if you've used your "free" limo service the night before. But some country inns offer dinners that are not only exquisite, but in an ambience that you can't get at a downtown restaurant. If you won the silent auction for a night at a resort or for a B&B, use the occasion of her birthday to celebrate in style.

The entire plan is to make her feel special. It is her special day; she is your special lady, so why not make it special? A card and a box of drug store chocolates just don't cut it, Charlie. If you have to be out of town on the day of her birthday, send her a big bouquet of flowers at work and include in the note a "rain check" for a special night together the following weekend or the first weekend you're able to be there. Don't assume anything or blow anything off. Women put a great deal of stake in how their man treats her on special days. It's not consciously a test, but subconsciously to them, it is. So make sure you pass yours with flying colors.

Christmas, like Thanksgiving is a day for people to spend with families. So, if you're not invited to her home on either, just chill.

She's not comfortable in her own mind fitting you into that milieu. Oftentimes, bright women who've come to a big city to become successful professionally are the "arbiters" in their families' numerous disputes back home. For them, holiday weekends are occasions of tremendous stress where they return to the old homestead and become listening posts for everyone to vent their side of the current family flap. Do you really want to be immersed in that stuff? I don't think so. When she's ready, she will announce to everyone ahead of time that she's bringing home her latest stiff, ah, er....her new boyfriend and for everyone to be on his/her best behavior. You won't even know about the little mini-cyclones that are buzzing around her as you struggle to learn everyone's name and where to park your carcass so as to be out of the way. Never get involved in any of those disputes, even if invited to do so. However, if your lady demands that you give your opinion, you would be wise to either stay above the fray or to at least take her side. If you don't, you may find yourself traveling back home alone.

Always take a hostess gift to your lady's mother. This is usually a nice potted plant (flowering or otherwise). If you feel like it, also take her dad a bottle of wine or a liqueur (never a bottle of hootch; inveterate scotch drinkers serve rotgut bourbon and vice versa, and you don't know which kind he likes). Gifts for the girlfriend at Christmas are always a dicey thing. Obviously, you don't want to give her anything too intimate in front of her family. And while popping the "question" in front of her whole family might seem swell in the movies, it is not recommended in real life. Dude, that's a very special thing between the two of you which should take place when the two of you are alone, and if that's how you really feel, Valentine's Day is only 52 days away!! Rather, an expensive sweater set, jewelry, or a rare book by her favorite author make great gifts at your first Christmas together. You'll also want to bring a small, inexpensive gift to give her parents, as well as for each of her siblings and any one else who's a permanent resident of the household. Other than for her parents, it need not be anything more than a $10 gift certificate from Starbucks, Blockbuster, or Barnes and Noble, but I once faced the embarrassment of not having a gift for an older sister of my lady who presented me with one. Oops!

If you're away from the family and are staying at one of your respective homes/apartments, the leeway is a bit broader, but again nothing too expensive if the relationship is less than three months old or if you're both not 100% sure that this thing between you is going somewhere.

New Year's Eve is for friends. I break down the New Year's Eve options into the following: the two of you home alone, as part of a larger group at a restaurant or club, at a friend's house with a large dinner crowd, or amidst the masses. I obviously prefer the first option. My favorite dish on this night is Spanish paella with rice, chicken, and seafood. It takes about an hour to prepare (see Appendix Three for the recipe), forty-five minutes to cook and cool, and a half-hour to consume with a good Spanish Barolo, so leave plenty of time before midnight so you don't come up short. Of course you can invite another couple or two but then, by necessity, it becomes far less of an intimate evening. The major reason I prefer to stay home is the obvious. You will want to enjoy fully the evening's offerings, and part and parcel of New Year's Eve is drinking (even if it's just the champagne as the ball drops). You always risk a major traffic ticket (or worse) afterwards driving home. If you attend a dinner party at a friend's house, I always prefer to bring the champagne (or the dinner wine), rather than having to bring a dish. Certainly I don't expect my lady to have to cook something to take to one of *my* friend's houses. Leave as shortly after midnight as is polite. The long-time married couples will be there until two or three. *You* have better things to take care of.

In short, while the holidays are a joyous time and offer opportunities to make your new relationship more meaningful and enriched, they also contain pitfalls for the archetypical male if he doesn't thoroughly think about them beforehand. Plan to come out of the holidays with your relationship more special than ever, as opposed to being tattered and in ruins.

Chapter Ten
Keep the Relationship Alive

"A woman, I always say, should be like a good suspense movie: The more left to the imagination, the more excitement there is. This should be her aim – to create suspense, to let a man discover things about her without her having to tell him."

Alfred Hitchcock

"Intimacy requires an ability to both merge and be separate, to come together and be apart, like oscillating on a giant swing from oneness to separateness, creating a constant rhythm."

Charlotte Kasl, *If the Buddha Dated*

As I've said earlier, the real killer of relationships is complacency and boredom, often caused by routine. So, you must be on your guard at all times to keep this from happening, to refrain from taking your relationship for granted. It is a natural thing for us humans to do; however, so you must continually take steps to prevent it.

All long-term successful relationships flourish because the two partners have grown and changed together as they have evolved as people. The old adage is true that unless you are growing, then you are receding. How are you growing? Besides the obvious (increasing your love and respect for each other more and more each day), the other growing, breathing thing is that you're changing together as each of you changes and, hopefully, matures. I had a friend onetime who told his friends that he fell in love with his wife all over again every single day. We were confused about what that meant or why he would have to do that, but hey, if it worked for him, go for it! Personally, I was reminded of him when that movie *50 First Dates* came out where the woman, because of a brain injury, couldn't remember anything that had happened to her from one day to the next so the guy who loved her had to get her to fall in love with him anew each and every day.

So, how do you keep your relationship from becoming stale? Well, many of the techniques and activities suggested in the chapter on keeping your relationship "fresh" certainly apply. You must keep your lives together interesting, as well as your sexual relationship. You should be empathetic toward each other's personal needs and towards the demands and necessities of each other's profession. If you demand that your partner always be with you outside the nine to five envelope, then you should really question whether it would be wise to strike up a relationship with an emergency room physician, a law enforcement officer, or a person in the military. If you require someone who's available to you during the day for some reason then there are many careers that simply do not afford that reality. If your partner is a tax accountant, then you should be prepared that from February to April 15 each year, he or she will be swamped with work. That's just a reality of that profession and you should be empathetic toward your lover in this regard.

You should keep the relationship fresh by showing appreciation and affection toward each other. I one time knew a chief operating officer who happened to have married the secretary of his boss, the chief executive officer. While this couple were both in their 60s, they went to lunch each day holding hands as if they were young teenagers. Not only was this cute, it was admirable as you just knew that there was no chance that their relationship would go stale. Why stop being flirtatious just because you're already a couple? Keep the magic alive. Never stop giving your lady compliments. Comment favorably when she gets a new haircut or an outfit. Never stop telling her how much you love her. Tell her how much you appreciate her and how happy she makes you. On a daily basis, either by email or by a phone call, ask her how her day is going. Let her know that you are thinking about her. When you talk to her, actually listen to what she's saying. Avoid the stereotype that men never really listen to what their women are saying to them. At least five minutes a day, give her complete, uninterrupted attention and during that period, express your appreciation for who she is and what she means to you. These sound pretty basic, but trust me they are among the first things to be forgotten when the "bloom is off" the new relationship. Key: never let the "bloom be off"!!

One way to deepen and enrich your relationship is for you to be a caring guy. Now, for some of us poor Neanderthals this may be hard, especially if we were raised in a super-male dominated household. What do I mean by this? It was common in my house while growing up to have numerous injuries. My brother and I were always playing sports and doing all kinds of physical and reckless things. So, scrapes, cuts, and worse were quite common. We were expected to "suck it up" and not be babies about it. Women weren't raised that way; most are not used to being physically injured. Now, this is slowly changing as more and more women are becoming active in sports, even contact sports, but many still are not. Therefore, if a woman gets hurt or has an operation, she expects her guy to give her comfort and to "be there" for her. I learned this the hard way. After experiencing more than one serious automobile crash, including one that literally took my leg, I could not relate to mundane, routine operations. I felt that such procedures were "ho hum." My first wife was a mentally tough lady, but was not used to pain. When she had a minor operation, I was too busy at my demanding job to put her procedure high up on my priority list. I screwed up and she never forgave me for it; nor should she have. But that's how I was raised. I am not rationalizing things or trying to excuse myself; that's just the way it was. But I was wrong. A lady should expect the guy in her life to be there for her, to care for her, to comfort her, and to ease the pain in any way he possibly can. If you do, you are properly doing your job as the man in your relationship.

Women need men who will listen about how their day went or what happened to them. All that's expected of the guy is to listen and make an occasional supportive comment, but by no means tell the woman how to solve the problem, unless the woman asks for suggestions or help.

Be adventurous. Try new things, both with respect to activities (ever been scuba diving or ballooning?) and with each other sexually. Be generous with each other, both in terms of material things and with respect to your time and attention. As well, be generous sexually; make your pleasure contingent upon her receiving pleasure, not just focusing on your getting off. Is the sex between you two becoming stale? Role play, pretend to be someone else, make a "blind" date and meet her in a public place as if you've just picked her up. Enjoy occasional erotic DVDs and read together things like *Penthouse Letters* not only to pick up new ideas but also to mutually excite yourselves.

Keep an optimistic attitude replete with a healthy and bounteous sense of humor. Have the capacity to laugh at each other in a non-threatening way and certainly with each other. View the world together with enthusiasm and vigor. Be fun to be with. Sure you have work problems, who doesn't? Suck it up. Don't be a whiner nor bring her down by always dragging out your professional problems to her. Sure if you need to vent, then vent. But don't do it all the time. It makes you a burden to be around. You want to keep her happy, and again one of the keys in doing so is your sense of humor. Your sense of humor can't shine through if you're always bitching about how unfair your boss is or how unreasonable your client is.

If your relationship has progressed to the point where you have moved in together, the probability that your interactions and sexual encounters will become routine goes way up. Get together with your calendars/Blackberries and schedule actual dates so that you *do not take each other for granted.* Just because you now live together is no reason that Friday night (or Saturday) still can't be "date night." Those little personal IOUs that I mentioned before become oh so much more important now. To the "gifts" previously mentioned you can now add in your IOUs that you will cook dinner for her, clean the bathroom, clean the refrigerator/oven, vacuum, make her breakfast in bed, paint the study, cut the grass, or any other chore that is tedious but necessary.

But most importantly, set mutual goals and write them down. It may sound hokey but many studies in both psychology and even business schools have shown that if you commit your goals to paper, you will more than likely attain them. Either put these written goals on the front of your refrigerator or on your bathroom or bedroom mirror. Why goals? Because, unless the two of you have mutual goals, then you're just drifting together. The goals can be material-oriented, professionally-related, or just personal. Lose twenty pounds can be a goal. Obtain partner. Buy a Mercedes 450 SL. Get elected to office. Take an around-the-world cruise. To be a legitimate goal, each should be attainable (the cruise is indeed attainable unless one of you is deathly afraid of being on the water or something like that), measurable, and should contain a date. "World peace," for example, would be both unattainable for an individual couple and by what date could you possibly put on that?

Many relationship counselors equate a good relationship with an "emotional bank account." Deposits are made into the account when the couple treat each other with love and respect. Withdrawals occur when one or both of the couple is rude, insensitive, selfish, or whatever. Sound relationships occur when continuous deposits grow the account and keep it vibrant and alive. Other experts suggest that "deposits" are made when the male partner: Spends time with her alone, listens to her deeply, touches her (non-sexually), accepts her unconditionally, is committed to her, encourages her with words, takes care of her financially, laughs with her, is her best friend, and keeps in mind the major idea – after God, but before all others, makes her his top priority. A woman's greatest need is for intimacy in which her partner shows and tells her that he knows and accepts her at the deepest level.

A word about fighting. Almost all normal and healthy relationships involve an occasional spat. The key is to fight fair and without being mean or demeaning. If you are losing the fight (and I mean verbal, never physical), keep the discussion on the matter at hand; don't change subjects to one on which you have the higher moral ground or the better arguments. That isn't fighting fairly. Stick to the topic in dispute and try not to let it get personal. It often does, but at least *try* to keep it to the logic of the matter in dispute and keep personal invectives to a minimum. Be on your guard against saying something that you will truly regret later. Criticize her position or her logic but don't call her names. Don't belittle her position, her intelligence, or her logic. Be angry but don't lose your respect for her and what you have together. Lastly, that old adage is oh so very true: try never to go to bed angry. Stay up all night if you have to, to resolve the issue. The threat of facing the next day with little sleep is incentive enough to reach a resolution. And there's little better sex than make-up sex!

Finally, you must be true to yourself. If you love her but you aren't happy, the responsibility is yours – not hers. It's not her fault that, say, you want someone to idolize you, and if she has decent self-esteem she probably cut that out within the first eight months of your relationship. So, if you really have needs that she isn't meeting, then it's best to cut bait, bub. However, before you make this irrevocable decision, does she really know what your needs are, or are you just assuming that she does? Be sure. Have a heart-to-heart, not in an accusatory tone, and let her know what you're missing. Chances are what you say will be a revelation to her and things will definitely improve; however, if she is disdainful or indifferent, then you know that letting her go is the right thing to do. As painful as it may be to do, do you really want to invest another five years into this relationship knowing that sooner or later you're going to cut her off at the knees and bail out? I've known people who have done that because it's just "easier" to go along in a kind of stupor and not hurt their partner, while all the time being truly unhappy. Be true to yourself, but having said that, you *must* also be honest with her. Remember, most people revert to their "true" selves two years into a relationship. The more honest you both are, the less likely there will be surprises between you. If you still love each other, despite the flaws and imperfections that we all have, the better chance you two will make it.

Good luck and happy loving!

Appendix One
Suggested Readings

Anderson, Colleen. "The New West Virginia One-Day Trip Book: More than 200 Affordable Adventures in the Mountain State," EPM Publications, McLean, VA, 1998.

Carlson, Richard. "The Don't Sweat Guide for Couples: 100 Ways to Be More Intimate, Loving and Stress-Free in Your Relationship," Don't Sweat Press, Orinda, CA, 2001.

Chase, Suzi Forbes, "Recommended Country Inns: Mid-Atlantic and Chesapeake Region, 9th Edition" Globe Pequot, Old Saybrook, CT, 2001.

Colbert, Judy and Ed. "Maryland Off the Beaten Path: A Guide to Unique Places," Globe Pequot Press, Chester, CT, 1990.

"The Complete Book of Chicken: Turkey, Game Hen, Duck, Goose, Quail, Squab, and Pheasant." Boston Common Press, New York, 1999.

Darling, Jennifer Dorland, Editor. "Better Homes and Gardens New Cook Book," Meredith Books, Des Moines, IA, 2002.

Gray, John. "Men are from Mars, Women are from Venus: A Practical Guide for Improving Communication and Getting What You Want in Your Relationships," Harper Collins, New York, 1992.

Hayes, Edward. "The Florida One-Day Trip Book: 52 Off Beat Excursions in and Around Orlando," EPM Publications, McLean, VA, 1990.

Hopkins, Martha and Randall Lockridge. "InterCourses: An Aphrodisiac Cookbook," Terrance Publishing, Waco, TX, 1997.

"The Innkeepers' Register, 12th Edition," Independent Innkeepers' Association, Marshall, MI, 2000.

Kane, Ariel. "How to Create a Magical Relationship," Ask Productions, Milford, NJ, 2006.

Kennedy, Doris and Duane Perreault. "Recommended Country Inns: Rocky Mountain Region: Colorado, Idaho, Montana, Nevada, Utah, Wyoming (6th Ed.)," Globe Pequot, Old Saybrook, CT, 1996.

Kramer, Matt. "Making Sense of Burgundy," William Morrow and Company, New York, 1990.

Lukacs, Paul. "The Great Wines of America: The Top Forty Vintners, Vineyards, and Vintages," W.W. Norton & Company, New York, 2005.

Marquis, June Harrington. "Weekends for Two: Places to Stay, Romantic Restaurants, Things to Do and See in the Mid-Atlantic Area," Liberty Publishing Company, Deerfield Beach, FL, 1989.

Mehta, Pushpendra. "The Game of Life & Relationships: Few are Prepared," eBook.com, London, 2006.

Mulligan, Tim. "Virginia: A History & Guide," Random House, New York, 1986.

Ockershausen, Jane. "One Day Nature Trips In and Around Washington: D.C. Beauty and Bounty," EPM Publications, McLean, VA, 1987.

Ockershausen, Jane. "The Georgia One-Day Trip Book: A New Way to Explore the State's Romantic Past, Vibrant Present, and Olympian Future," EPM Publications, McLean, VA, 1993.

Ockershausen, Jane. "The Maryland One-Day Trip Book: 200 Day-Long Excursions through America in Miniature," Howell Press, Charlottesville, VA, 1999.

Ockershausen, Jane. "The New Virginia One-Day Trip Book: From the Mountains to the Sea, Six Geographic Centers Offer 375 Scenic, Historic and Recreational Delights," EPM Publications, McLean, VA, 1996.

Ockershausen, Jane. "The New Washington One-Day Trip Book: 101 Offbeat Excursions in and Around the Nation's Capital," EPM Publications, McLean, VA, 1992.

Ockershausen, Jane. "The North Carolina One-Day Trip Book: Land of Dramatic Diversity," EPM Publications, McLean, VA, 1990.

Ockershausen, Jane. "The South Carolina One-Day Trip Book: Short Journeys to History, Charm and Adventure in the Palmetto State," EPM Publications, McLean, VA, 1998.

Paananean, Eloise. "The Baltimore One-Day Trip Book: A New View of What to Do in and Around the All-American City," EPM Publications, McLean, VA, 1985.

Parker, Robert M., Jr. "Bordeaux: The Definitive Guide for the Wines Produced Since 1961," Simon and Schuster, New York, 1985, 1991, and 1998.

Parker, Robert M., Jr. "Parker's Wine Buyer's Guide," Simon and Schuster, New York, 2002.

Ramsdale, David and Cynthia W. Gentry. "Red Hot Tantra," Fair Winds Press, Glouchester, MA, 2004.

Richo, David. "How to be an Adult in Relationships: The Five Keys to Mindful Loving," Random House, New York, 2002.

Sampson, Val. "Tantra between the Sheets: The Easy and Fun Guide to Mind-Blowing Sex," Ulysses Press, Berkeley, 2003.

Smith, Jane Ockershausen. "One Day Trips Through History: 200 Excursions Within 150 Miles of Washington, D.C.," EPM Publications, McLean, VA, 1982.

Smith, Jane Ockershausen. "The Philadelphia One-Day Trip Book: 101 Exciting Excursions in and Around the City," EPM Publications, McLean, VA, 1985.

Squier, Elizabeth and Eleanor Berman. "Recommended Country Inns: New England, 19th Edition," Globe Pequot, Old Saybrook, CT, 2006.

Thalimer, Carol and Dan. "Recommended Country Inns: The South, 8th Edition," Globe Pequot, Old Saybrook, CT, 2001.

Welwood, John. "Perfect Love, Imperfect Relationships: Healing the Wound of the Heart," Trumpter Press, New York, 2007.

Whiston, Lionel. "Are You Fun to Live With?" Word Books, Waco, TX, 1970.

"Wine Spectator's Ultimate Guide to Buying Wine: Eighth Edition," Wine Spectator Press, New York, 2004.

Zraly, Kevin. "Windows on the World Complete Wine Course," Sterling Publishing Co., New York, 2006.

Appendix Two
Collecting Wine

To collect wine, all you need is a dark closet, hopefully on an interior wall of your house or apartment. The most important things for storing wine are darkness, a stable temperature less than 70 degrees, and smoothness (not getting jostled or bumped or subject to constant vibrations). Just make sure the bottles are lying down to ensure that there is no air pocket beneath the cork, and the closet is not too dry (this is why basement closets are better if you have one). You want the bottom of the cork covered in wine, so lay the bottles flat or slightly canted toward the bottles' openings. If you store wine above 70 degrees, you must drink it within two years or it will likely go bad. Below that, a warmer (65-70 degrees) space just means that the wine will age and mature faster. If you keep it too cool, it will never properly age and your grandchildren will taste the wine at its peak, not you. However, other than great Bordeaux or California Cabernet Sauvignons most wine is best drunk young, rather than aged. By young, I mean after a year, unless it is Beaujolais, which is designed to be drunk immediately.

You can make a homemade wine cabinet by stacking up plywood and bricks, or get some simple and inexpensive ones made of pine from a store like Ikea. As an alternative to keeping your wine in a closet, put it in a wine cabinet. Good wine cabinets are now available for less than $2000 that are of sufficient size and quality wherein you can store 20 cases or more in a fine wooden cabinet that matches the highest quality furniture. My own is by Dometic. I like it because it is cooled by a patented system that does not vibrate (which all motors do to some extent), which is not good for wine.

If you're really serious about wine, check with the major wine stores in your area about buying some Bordeaux futures. There is nothing nebulous or mysterious about wine futures (unlike some other commodities). Basically, it involves purchasing a case of wine two years before it arrives. The major wine press (e.g., Wine Advocate, Wine Spectator) tastes the nascent wines directly from the barrel (prior to their being bottled) and with their long years of experience are able to predict accurately which ones will be outstanding in two years. Now, you might say, "I'm not giving *anyone* my money two years before I even get to taste the stuff. That's crazy!" Well, stay broke, my friend. I had one friend who bought sufficient cases of 1982 (at that time the greatest vintage since the unmatched 1945) First Growth Bordeaux to fund his children's college educations! So where would you keep them? If you don't have a wine cabinet, closet, or cellar, there are usually reputable wine storage units rentable for such purposes. I bought several bottles of that same vintage for under $80 and am now enjoying them with special meals. The cost to obtain them now? Even if you could find available bottles from the 1982 vintage, they would cost $500-1300 per bottle.

In 1855, the French government (I know, I know, but bear with me here for a moment) classified the top 60 chateaux in Bordeaux into first, second, third, fourth, and fifth growths (it's different in Bordeaux – with the exception of the St. Emilion district east of the Gironde River – than the Cru and Grand Cru system used in Burgundy). Only four wines were named to the First Growth: Lafite Rothschild, Latour, Margaux, and Haut Brion. Since then, there has only been one change to that list: in 1973 Mouton Rothschild was added. There are fourteen wines contained in the Second Growth list, the top four or five of which are known as the "super seconds." Of these, included is my favorite Bordeaux of all: Pichon-Longueville, Comtesse de Lalande, commonly known as Pichon Lalande. It costs literally one-half as much as the First Growths, and I've hosted blind tastings where everyone present picked the Pichon as his/her favorite over Lafite Rothschild, hands down! It is a hearty, meaty wine and while not as tannic as its literal neighbor Latour, is round and delicious. Robert Parker, the Maryland-based wine tasting expert with the iron palette ranks practically every wine for sale in the U.S. every year. His 0 to 100 rankings are followed world-wide to distinguish plonk from the really good stuff, and any wine ranked over 90 is considered outstanding. Between 1978 and 1983, Pichon averaged 91.7 following behind only the distinguished (and expensive) Chateau Margaux for average ratings.

These are the only wines I would suggest you considering buying as futures. You will pay a couple of thousand dollars per case (around $200/bottle), but trust me, when the wine arrives in two years you won't be able to touch it for twice that amount. It's better appreciation than putting money in a CD or the stock market. Most Americans will never taste a mature Bordeaux. They either drink what they do buy way too early, or they can't afford to buy a mature bottle when it is at its peak perfection. With futures, you avoid both those shortcomings.

There are also several California Cabernet Sauvignons that have reached this pinnacle and of which I would consider buying as futures. These include Mondavi Reserve (a Reserve is where the vintner reserves only the very best grapes for those bottles), Silver Hill, Caymus Special Selection, Mayacamas, Dunn, Montelena, Stag's Leap, and Heitz Martha's Vineyard. In my opinion, the two best wines made in America are Dominus and Opus One, which parenthetically, are both made in the Bordeaux style, i.e., they are a mix of Cabernet Sauvignon, Cabernet Franc, and Merlot grapes. Most California Cab are just that, and usually a bit too tannic (the drying phenomenon left on your tongue – the pucker factor – that comes from the wine's exposure to the leaves and stems before being put in the barrel) for my taste. The other two grapes round and soften the Cabernet Sauvignon.

Before I discuss the major varieties of wines available today, let me share a couple of secrets about serving wine. Most Americans drink their red whites too hot and their white wines too cold. The result is that the true, often complex flavors are masked. The trick is to put the red wine you are serving in the refrigerator for 20 or 30 minutes prior to serving it and to take the white wine out of the refrigerator a half hour before pouring. The result will be that you will serve your guests the wine in its optimum condition to best show off its qualities. Additionally, for a red Bordeaux or California Cabernet, uncork it at least an hour before you serve it. The air mixing with the wine lets it "breathe" and oxidizes it to soften the remaining tannins, again, allowing the wine to be tasted at its zenith. The best cabernet sauvignons that I have tasted come from magnums (containing two normal-sized bottles) or larger sized bottles. For some reason, fine wines age even better in the larger-sized bottles, the largest of which contains 20 bottles of wine.

Is your red wine too young? A notable Bordeaux wholesaler taught me a great trick one time at a tasting of brand new Bordeaux. I told him at the outset that I was totally prepared to be under-whelmed by the brand new Bordeaux he was serving. When he queried why, I told him that the wine was far too young to be any good. Then he told me not to worry and showed me the trick taught him by a famous sommelier: for every time you decant a red wine (i.e., pour it from the bottle into a decanter), the wine is aged one year. Therefore, a brand new Bordeaux or cabernet will taste four years old (usually close to its normal prime) if you pour it from the bottle into a decanter once and then from decanter to decanter three more times. Parenthetically, I used to attend a great many wine tastings to learn about new wines, and I usually bought a case of my favorite wine tasted at that event. In this manner, there is no struggle to recall later what wine I most enjoyed.

For whites, the key for drinking wine with fish and shell fish is to drink a crisp, dry, steely wine that was stored in stainless steel barrels. Usually this means a Sauvignon Blanc (white Bordeaux are almost exclusively made with this grape), a Pouilly-Fume, a Sancerre, or a Fume Blanc (Sauvignon Blanc grown in California). Some people don't like their white wine quite as dry as these gravelly wines. If so, try a Murphy-Goode Fume Blanc from California which is so rich and creamy, it borders on a chardonnay. Chenin Blanc is a touch sweeter than Sauvignon Blanc and is excellent with most seafood. It comes most often from Vouvray from central France and from California.

The white wine of choice for many Americans has become chardonnay, the grape from which France's incredible white Burgundies are made. However, because of that popularity the prices have been driven upwards. When varietals (wine identified by its primary grape composition) first became popular, we were confused as many California winemakers were selling Chablis. This was, however, a mix of any old white grape in jug bottles. True Burgundian Chablis is a chardonnay from one of the five districts of Burgundy which lend their name to the grapes grown therein. Everyone is familiar with the name Montrachet in Burgundy. There are, however, seven types of Montrachets produced in Burgundy (actually, the Cote d' Or), depending on which particular village and which part of the slope on which grew the grapes. There are some 1000 chateaus in Bordeaux, the grapes from a particular chateau go into that particular wine only, and no other grapes are allowed to be included. In Burgundy, the grapes for a dozen or more different labels may grow on the same slope of ground. Therefore, it is far more complicated to track where the grapes in any particular bottle came from, but trust me it is closely regulated by the French Institut National des Appellations d'Origine des Vins.

The most well-known white Burgundies made from chardonnay are Chablis, Meursault, Corton-Charlemagne, Montrachet, Puligny-Montrachet, Chevalier-Montrachet, Batard-Montrachet, and Chassagne-Montrachet. However, there are literally dozens more. For each of these, there may be a dozen or two vineyards authorized to use the name on their labels. In the U.S., California makes truly world-class chardonnay wine as well. South Africa, Chile, Argentina, New Zealand, and Australia are catching up. Of the100 top wines released in 2006, the *Wine Spectator* included seven chardonnays, five from California and one each from Washington State (Chateau Ste. Michelle) and Australia. Chardonnay is simply scrumptious with fowl (although a good pinot noir also goes well with turkey). A rich, buttery, oaky chardonnay will match pork and light meats perfectly or rich casseroles. The oak taste comes from being stored for at least a year in rich oaken barrels that impart some of their taste to the wine. Unlike the Sauvignon Blanc grape, the best chardonnays are rich, creamy, and complex and extremely pleasant tasting on the palette. Citrus and fruit flavors come through strongly.

Most chardonnays should be drunk between 1 and 3 years old. Any younger, and they taste "green," clearly too young. Beyond that and they begin to turn. The first hint is that the crisp, fruity taste is "off." Later, it turns first to sherry (and the color turns coppery), and then to vinegar. However, French chardonnays usually last 5 to 10 years, and one California chardonnay which is extremely hard to get as it rarely appears in retail stores (Stony Hill) doesn't begin drinking well for three years and lasts easily for 7-8 years. I once attended a blind tasting of 25 chardonnays with 40 people. The wines were all from California, save for one expensive white Burgundy and one from Virginia. Every person at the tasting but me chose this one wine as his/her favorite (it was my second favorite). For the one I picked I would have bet a month's salary that it was the French Burgundy, but it turned out to be a $12 California (Cambria). The one everyone else picked was Naked Mountain from Front Royal, VA. I've since bought a case every year (less than $20/bottle) but you must drink it within a year or it goes bad.

For spicy food (Chinese, Thai, etc. – not Mexican, which should only be eaten with either beer, sangria, or margaritas), you should pick up a good Gewurtzraminer. True Gerz (as it's called) is a unique blend of sweetness and spice. If you don't get a good one, all you taste is the former. Buy only the French (Alsace) offerings. But for $15-20, you can get one which balances the two tastes perfectly. It matches the spice in the above mentioned cuisines exquisitely. A good Riesling from Germany might also fit.

The movie *Sideways* blew holes in the nation's consumption of merlot, a red grape that I prefer as a moderator of the harsh taste of young cabernets. However, it is a decent, lower priced wine that has its followers and fits with many meat dishes.

Syrah or shiraz is a moderately-priced red grape that often tastes spicy or peppery. It is usually drinkable at a young age and affords those on a modest budget to enjoy top-flight wine at a reasonable price. Of the *Wine Spectator's* top 100 wines from 2006, ten were of this varietal (two were multiple-blends), mostly from Australia.

Fourteen of the *Wine Spectator's* top 2006-released wines were Pinot Noir's. Although this grape made its splash on the world stage by being the basis of the most expensive wines in the world (French Burgundy rouge), not one of those 14 was from Burgundy. Most were from California, although four were from Oregon. Pinot Noir is usually ready to drink at an earlier age than is cabernet; it is usually characterized as bright, feminine and berry-like. *New* releases of this wine from Burgundy average about $50 but can reach as high as $460. The price only climbs as the wine matures and becomes more drinkable. Pinot Noir is a difficult grape to grow, and vineyards in California have struggled to grow quality grapes. Lately the ones from Sonoma County have shown great results. However, year in and year out the best Pinots made in America are those from Oregon. I one time attended a private wine tasting comprised of experienced wine drinkers/collectors. It was a blind tasting of Pinot Noirs. Of twenty wines, only one was not from Burgundy, but it was everyone's favorite, and it was from Oregon (Domaine Drouhin). The next morning, a Saturday, every single one of us was present at the only local wine store that sold that label. We bought them out. Pinot Noir is great with meat dishes and must be drunk before it is ten years old; however, the older the wine, the simpler the dish should be so as not to overpower it.

Zinfandel is the only truly American grape (most Bordeaux wines are offspring of American cabernet sauvignon grapes that were planted after most of the French vines were killed by the phllox, but those American transplants were, in turn, progeny of French cuttings). Zinfandel is a massive wine, almost black in color and possessing a high alcoholic content. It is reasonably-priced, ready-to-drink and delicious. It is best drunk prior to reaching about eight years old and is best with beef entrees. White zin is made from the red grape, the juice of which is not allowed to remain in contact with the grape skins for very long, so it comes out rose in color.

Chateauneuf-du-Pape is an appellation in France's Rhone Valley that makes a wide variety of wines from thinner Beaujolais-style to jammy, fruity wines that can be rich and full-bodied, lasting 20 years. Of the top 100 wines of 2006, the *Wine Spectator* ranks four of the top 19 as Chateauneuf-du-Pape. There are a few (7%) Chateauneuf-du-Pape that are white, but most are deep red wines costing a minimum of $25/bottle. They are great with turkey and veal. They offer a cheaper alternative to Bordeaux.

Another red grape that has become quite popular is Malbec. A handful of California vintners have made outstanding and reasonably-priced Malbec for over a decade; however, the new rage in the wine world is the tremendous amount of sales of Malbecs from Argentina ranging from $8 to $50 per bottle.

Spain, Italy, and Germany make thousands of wines. Some are excellent, especially the best Barolos from Italy and the formidable Riojas from Spain. Both are usually loaded with tannin and must be aged several years and decanted for hours to be approachable. However, there is nothing better with Italian tomato sauces than chianti. The best chiantis, however, are not contained in bottles wrapped in straw.

Champagne is the only appropriate wine for certain occasions (buying a new house, birthdays, engagements, weddings, etc.). Champagne cannot be served too cold, and it should be opened by holding tightly to the cork and *turning the bottle*. People who open champagne by letting the cork bounce around the room (and injuries to people are more common that you would think) are crazy. Only champagnes coming from the Champagne area of France can legally be called champagne; the rest are "sparkling wines." Vintage champagnes, those that actually contain a date, vary widely from year to year and will age nicely if properly stored. Other champagnes should be drunk young. Not every year deserves to be named as a vintage year, so when that is the case, the vineyard does not denote that year's grapes as a vintage and mixes the harvest with those from other vineyards or even those from other years. The best champagne is *not* Dom Perignon! I have taken wine novices to champagne tastings and, like the Pichon v. Lafite example above, they are blown away when they taste a half dozen champagnes that are far superior to Dom Perignon which Hollywood has put on a pedestal it doesn't necessarily deserve. My favorite is the almond-tasting rose, Louis Roeder Cristal; however, its price and availability severely limits the opportunities to enjoy it. However, you do not need to spend more than $50 (retail) to enjoy a really great bottle of champagne; at restaurants, of course, you'll have to pay more. Check the list below for some great, reasonably-priced bubbly. Most French champagne houses have two or three different labels priced at various levels. If it's not a vintage champagne, the sooner you drink a bottle, the better. Fine vintage champagnes can last 25 years. Most champagne is made from chardonnay (Blanc de Blancs) but some is actually produced from Pinot Noir. Most people connect champagne drinking with either parties or before a dinner; however, I have learned that the most pleasurable champagne drinking can be had when it is consumed with dessert, especially a chocolate one!

Additional after dinner dessert wines are available from Sauterne in Bordeaux and from vintage Portuguese port. While your grandparents might equate port with the tawny ports as an aperitif like sherry, vintage port is in a far-different league. Between 1950 and 1999 in only nine years were the port grapes judged of sufficiently high quality to be declared a vintage. Those wines, after a decade of aging, offer the after-dinner drinker an incredibly enjoyable experience. The fortified wine is literally intense with a powerful nose and complex flavors. It is drunk from snifters to afford the maximum opportunity to whiff the delightful aromas. Powerful and rich are adjectives used to describe the best. Year-after-year the best producers are Dow, Fonseca, Graham, Quinta do Noval, and Taylor. You can buy a top notch vintage port, upon release, for $25-50, and that bottle will last for 50 years. Forty year old port sells for a fraction of the price of a Bordeaux or Burgundy counterpart from the same year. Lay them away for ten years, and then open about one a month during the winter, and life will be good. I actually prefer to drink port in the hot tub or Jacuzzi rather than brandy, as despite the fact that they're both fortified, only the latter will give you a headache. You know how sometimes legends are way overrated? I thought the legend about drinking vintage port accompanied by Stilton cheese and walnuts was one of those. Boy, was I wrong! The three tastes go together as if they were literally invented for each other.

Most people cannot possibly imagine drinking sweet white wine; however, I make an exception for good Sauterne. Made in the Barsac and Sauternes region 25 miles south of the city of Bordeaux, this intensely rich and elegant white wine is superb as a dessert wine. Although a great harvest only occurs about three times a decade, you can buy a decent Sauterne for around $40; however, you must cellar it for at least four or five years. After that prepare yourself: it tastes like honey on the palette. Only a great Madiera can top it, but good Madiera, from the Portuguese-owned island off that coast is even cheaper than good port.

I hope that the foregoing offers a glimpse into the world of wine. A full appreciation of the fruit of the vine goes hand-in-hand with the love of a special woman. Wine smoothes over difficulties in the rough spots that appear in any relationship and offers a perfect way to wind down together after a stressful workweek. Recent medical evidence also has shown the long term beneficial effects of wine drinking, especially imbibing red wine. Elements contained in red wines serve to help minimize the build up of plaque in the arteries. A glass or two daily can only prolong your life. Enjoying wine need not entail purchasing a second mortgage on your home; however, with a modest investment one can enjoy the maximum benefits of wine.

Recommended wines that consistently are of high quality at *reasonable* expense (wines are listed in random order and are from California unless otherwise denoted):

Whites
Chardonnays
Cambria
ZD
Cakebread
Ferrari-Carano Reserve
Kistler
Kalin
Silverado
Naked Mountain (VA)
Chateau St. Michelle (WA)
Mt. Eden Reserve
Frog's Leap
Kendall-Jackson Reserve

Sauvignon Blancs

Ferrari-Carano
Mason Cellars
Mondavi Fume Blanc
Murphy-Goode Fume Blanc
Konocti Fume Blanc
Kalin

Reds
Cabernet/Bordeaux
Mondavi Reserve
Napa Ridge
Arrowood
Hess Collection
Napa Ridge
J. Pedroncelli
Beringer
Barboursville (VA)
Caymus
Dunn
Flora Springs
Potensac (FR)
Duhart Milon (FR)
Cousino Macul Reserve (Chile)
Los Vascos (Chile)
Poujeaux (FR)
Veyry (FR)

Pinot Noirs
Domaine Drouhin(OR)
DomaineSerene(OR)
Shea (OR)
Domaine Alfred
Lemelson (OR)
Saintsbury
Mountain View

Champagnes/Sparkling Wines
Ken Wright (OR)
Kistler
Bollinger Special Cuvee (FR)
Veuve Clicquot (yellow label)(FR)
Louis Roederer Brut Premier (FR)
Pol Roger (FR)
Piper Heidsieck (FR)
Bruno Paillard (FR)
Iron Horse
Roederer Estate
Domaine Chandon Reserve
Jordan J

Zinfandel
Ravenswood (esp. the Reserve)
Turley Cellars

Appendix Three
Paella Recipe

This recipe has served as many as six people. When I've served only two or four, I've frozen the rest for a wonderful, last second dinner on a busy weeknight when there wasn't time to cook anything from scratch. Happy eating!

Buy:
6 Langostino lobster tails
6 medium sized-raw shrimps in their shells
6 small hard-shelled clams
6 mussels
3 Spanish (or in a pinch, South American) chorizo sausages
6 small, boneless chicken breasts
2 t salt
Fresh ground black pepper
½ cup olive oil
2 oz lean boneless pork (salt pork is best), chop into ½ inch cubes
½ cup finely chopped Spanish onions (or use the dried onion flakes though not as tasty)
1 t finely chopped garlic (can use bottled prepared garlic)
1 each medium-sized sweet red, yellow, and green peppers, seeded,

de-ribbed and cut into 1 ½ by ¼ inch wide strips
1 large tomato, peeled, seeded and finely chopped (or use large can of chopped tomatoes but try to remove the seeds)
3 cups raw medium or long-grain rice (get from the Spanish/Latino supermarket)
¼ t ground saffron or saffron threads (from same market); pulverize with mortar and pestle or with the back of a spoon (this is *the* most expensive spice but makes the dish!)
6 c boiling water (put in a tea kettle, bring to a boil, then put on warm so when you need it, it doesn't take forever to boil)
½ cup frozen peas (thoroughly defrosted)
2 lemons, cut lengthwise into wedges
Paper towels
Wine (to drink while you're cooking)

Shell the shrimp, but leave the tails on and de-vein them. Scrub the shellfish and remove the black, ropelike tufts from the mussels. Set all three aside.

Put the sausages in a large skillet and prick them with a fork several times. Cover them with enough water to submerge them and bring to a boil over high heat; then lower the heat and simmer them for 5 minutes. Drain them on paper towels and set aside after cutting them into ¼ inch rounds.

Pat the chicken breasts dry with paper towels and season with 1 t of salt and pepper. Heat ¼ c of olive oil over high heat until a light haze forms above it. Carefully tong in the chicken, skin side down, and brown well, turning constantly and browning consistently without burning. As each browns remove them onto paper towels.

Add lobster to the remaining oil and turn frequently over high heat until the shell turns pinkish orange. Set them aside on a plate and add the sausages to the pan, browning quickly on both sides. Then set them aside on paper towels to drain.

Discard that oil and in the same large skillet, add the remaining ¼ c of olive oil and heat until a light haze forms above it. Add the salt pork and brown it quickly on all sides over high heat. Add the onions, garlic, pepper strips, and tomato. Stirring constantly, cook this briskly until most of the moisture is gone and the mixture is thick. This is called the *sofrito*. Set it aside.

About 30 minutes before you plan to serve the paella, pull the top rack out of the oven and preheat the oven to 400 degrees. In a 14-inch paella pan or casserole (I use a dutch oven) at least 14 inches wide and 2 ½ inches deep combine the *sofrito*, rice, 1 t of salt, and saffron. Pour in the boiling water and while stirring constantly, bring to a boil over high heat. As soon as it boils, quickly remove it from the heat. Arrange the chicken, lobster, sausage, shrimp, clams, and mussels on top of the rice and scatter the peas randomly.

Set the casserole on the bottom rack of the oven and bake for 30 minutes or until all the liquid has been absorbed by the rice. *Never* stir the dish once you put it in the oven. Pull the casserole out of the oven when done, and if your serving of the dish is delayed by whatever reason simply lay a kitchen towel over the top to keep it warm. But do let it rest for about 10 minutes before serving. Garnish with lemons on each diner's plate. I prefer dishing it onto plates still in the kitchen and carrying them into the dining room. Serve with a salad of lettuce and cherry tomatoes with Italian dressing and a nice Spanish Rioja. Serve flan, Spanish custard, for dessert.

Lightning Source UK Ltd.
Milton Keynes UK
UKOW05f2003091213

222686UK00008B/647/P